Joining Music with Reason

Joining Music with Reason

34 Poets, British and American
Oxford 2004–2009

chosen by

Christopher Ricks

WAYWISER

First published in 2010 by

THE WAYWISER PRESS

Bench House, 82 London Road, Chipping Norton, Oxfordshire OX7 5FN, UK
P.O. Box 6205, Baltimore, MD 21206, USA
http://waywiser-press.com

A CIP catalogue record for this book is available from the British Library

ISBN 978-1-904130-40-6

Printed and bound by
T J International Ltd., Padstow, Cornwall, PL28 8RW

Contents

Preface: Joining Music with Reason

Dr Johnson couched his high praise of poetry in these terms, and with reason, in *The Rambler* No. 86 (12 January 1751): 'The poet has this peculiar superiority, that to all the powers which the perfection of every other composition can require, he adds the faculty of joining music with reason, and of acting at once upon the senses and the passions.'

He, to whom one adds *she*.

Himself (as we say) a poet, Johnson stands among the greatest within the superb English tradition of the poet-critic. Ben Jonson, Dryden, Pope, Johnson, Wordsworth, Coleridge, Keats, Arnold, T.S. Eliot, Robert Graves, W.H. Auden, William Empson, Donald Davie, Geoffrey Hill: the line is something more than distinguished since it is variously distinctive, markedly individual. Some of these poet-critics have graced both Oxford and the art of poetry as the Professor of Poetry, being for many of us its finest exemplars: Arnold, Graves, Auden.... But the Professorship is neither a chair in creative writing nor a dais from which to read one's own poems, and for more than three centuries the Professorship of Poetry has not been limited to those whom Eliot liked drily to call *practitioners*. Respect should of course be paid to a tradition-within-the-tradition that has been established since the Second World War, by which a *practising poet* is held to have a special claim. But there has never been a holder of the post who proved more illuminating and more eloquent than A.C. Bradley a century ago; likewise, thirty years ago, the art of poetry gained much from the passionate acumen of John Jones, no poet but a critic whose understanding of Wordsworth and of Keats (and of Aristotle) made manifest what it is for the art of criticism to join music with reason.

No poet myself, and moreover someone who does not write or publish poems, I was honoured (not sure about *humbled*, much on the lips of newly-elected politicians) by election to the Professorship. Conscious of responsibilities to poetry new as well as old, I decided that there should be a poetry reading, every term for the five years, at which a poet of Oxford (either as in Oxford now or as having a recent Oxford affiliation) would be joined by a poet from America. (I have taught for more than twenty years at Boston University.) This collection brings together the work, love's labours won, of all these poets. Fifteen occasions, so thirty poets, one would have thought, which means that it does need to be explained why here are *34 Poets, British and American, Oxford 2004-2009*. Simply, that David Ferry was the American poet for both the first and the last of the readings at Balliol College, in tribute to his enduring friendship and his enduring achievement as poet and translator; that on one occasion I was fortunately able to recruit three Oxford poets; and that on the final occasion, in Trinity 2009, I chose to substitute for an Oxford poet my reading poems (mostly early poems) by five Oxford poets of the 1950s who had meant much to me then and who still do: Geoffrey Hill, Elizabeth Jennings, Adrian Mitchell, Jonathan Price, and Anthony Thwaite, all of whose art and generosity constitute the coda to this anthology.

Poems speak for themselves as well as for and to their readership, and in any case it would be folly for me to try to *encapsulate* what are by no means capsules and what, being good poems, are as various as life itself. In my introduction to the *New Oxford Book of Victorian Verse* twenty years ago, I found that I was as much warning myself as warning others about the perils of an introduction. Taste, discretion, and decision have, one likes to think, been exercised so as to make manifest the variety of poetry, and then the work of variety is to be pre-emptively undone in an introduction, flattened into a summary of what is to be found in the ensuing pages. 'To Generalize is to be an Idiot', wrote William Blake, generalizing with the best of us. 'To Particularize is the Alone Distinction of Merit'.

'Being himself a poet', reports Boswell, à propos of the fortunate College, 'Johnson was peculiarly happy in mentioning how many of the sons of Pembroke were poets; adding, with a smile of sportive triumph, "Sir, we are a nest of singing birds."' Sportive triumph is the thing, or is one of the things. The choice of poets was mine, assisted imaginatively by friends better acquainted with Oxford than I have become over the years.

Except within the coda, the choice of the poems was the poets'. Ten pages each, please, with a welcome to translations as well as to the many other forms that poetry may take. My gratitude is owed to the poets themselves; to Balliol College, handsome as ever; to the University of Oxford's pre-electronicized voters, Masters of Arts (those were the days that are no more); to Erica Zimmer, who helped me with bringing the book about; and to Philip Hoy and Waywiser Press for being so good as to hail and realize the enterprise.

Christopher Ricks

April 2010

SUSAN BARBOUR

Susan Barbour grew up in Champaign, Illinois. She holds a BA from Dartmouth, an MA from Johns Hopkins, and an MSt from Oxford where she will be reading for a DPhil at Somerville College. Her poetry and criticism have appeared in British and American journals. Currently living in Paris, Susan is completing her first book of poetry, which explores the model-artist transaction, as well as an experimental memoir. She is a certified sommelier and author of the wine blog Savvy Sippers. The poem 'There' first appeared in *Oxford Poetry*. (Photo courtesy of Faith Barter.)

Caedmon, Draw Me Something

and then body spoke I breathed in preverbal proverbs only
slower nudity and light were irreducible were impulses down
my arm
onto carbon in space

whatever I thought was
spirit was
thoughtless thought in
optical and proper volar digital nerves

The Gray Area

I first tried writing at four. I did not get very far, because my S's looked like this: Ƨ. I then tried writing with my left hand: rubbish. My mother, who wrote her dissertation on childhood literacy, presented me with a pack of phonics flashcards. I got three wrong, pitched the sounds across the room, then returned to drawing flora and fauna. At ten, I noticed that my bunnies looked like amorphous distant cousins of the possum. This, according to cognitive scientists, is the age when the brain becomes *lateralized*. The left, analytical side develops rapidly and proceeds to dissect and judge the work of the right, visual side as inaccurate and flawed. Names and categories intercept perceptions of values and edges. At this point the child must make a choice between favoring the visual, holistic, and perceptual side or the verbal, linear, and analytical one. Girls, it is noted, have acute body awareness (their drawings exhibit more parts), and, cognizant of their figurative disparities, quit drawing sooner. Perhaps owing to patience (for which I was once awarded the Bus-Stop Award at Girl Scout Camp – the value of which seemed to me discredited by persistent reminders that patience *is* a virtue) or, more likely, to a degree of impudence (I once famously kicked a curio cabinet after overhearing my grandmother tell my mother that I was too young to be sitting next to breakables), I disobeyed the tyrannical left brain and protracted the painful penitence of drawing badly while simultaneously learning how to read and write. I chose not to choose. Between the two cerebral hemispheres is a mass of nervous tissue, a bridge, known as the corpus callosum (Latin: tough body). According to a 1992 article in *Science*, this structure is larger in women. This sexual dimorphism has since been challenged, however, recent studies do seem to suggest that the area is significantly larger in musicians than in non-musicians. At twenty-seven, I went deaf in my left ear, which meant I could no longer locate sounds in space. This amounted to a curious reversal of the aural equivalent of the painter's age-old problem: how to divine a third dimension when limited to only two? It also compounded my left-right confusion. I used to visualize the multi-colored map in the backseat of NYC taxi-cabs while facing North so as to discern east from west. Incidentally, my first apartment there was located at 29th and Third. In the backseat taxi-cab map (now supplanted by GPS), this area was grey and had no name. You can imagine my relief when my fourth grade art teacher told me that *grey* could equally be spelled with an *a*.

Minerva

I needed the pocket money is what I ended up telling people. But choices get made about what ought to be illumined. The light gets trapped where it might have been refracted. Evergreen Video, now out of business, was located on Carmine Street, a three minute walk from my apartment. One afternoon I grabbed *La Belle Noiseuse* because of the cover. I turned it over and read *When he encounters the beautiful and fascinating Marianne (Emmanuelle Beart), he is inspired to return to the unfinished canvas, using her as his new model. But disturbing tensions develop as the work progresses and the reasons for the painting's original rejection begin to surface.* The first three art schools I called were closed for the summer. When I called a life drawing studio on Spring Street a woman picked up. Have you done this before she said. No I said. Well do you draw she said. Yes, I lied, I mean not in a while but I have. Well come into the studio at six tonight and I'll give you some charcoal and some paper. You can see what the model does and if you think you can do it after that we can speak. As a model you'll get to draw for free. Ask for me, Minerva. Thanks I said. I could really use the money.

from *Quick Poses*

I measure time
in charcoal scratches

they are more real to me
than the knots in my back

one minute one pose
twenty poses sixty seconds each
Minerva calls *begin*

the back ripples
as if uncertain, as if
it doesn't approve

of its audience
yet. it settles,
keenly remembers itself

as spine – head to buttocks –
the *S* curve
begs contact

this is not the touching
that vanishes
when lovers part

no. this back
asks to be memorized
it begs to be

a relic of touch:
the element between

my moving hand
and paper

with my right hand
I reach for the light on my face

from the ball of my left foot
a prayer moves up, streaks through
my body's diagonal

and before it finds my outstretched hand,
it slips

out of my eye

my eraser

is wiser than
I: it draws

the still invisible out

Metaxu

I

Metaxu means between. In Plato's *Symposium,* men get drunk and take turns riffing on the nature of love. Hetaerae could come, but wives were not invited. I have personally never enjoyed Greek wine except some whites in the summertime. Socrates gives the last speech. His speech is deemed the best, because he tells the story of Diotima, the prophetess who told him while drawing well water that Love was the daughter of Poverty and Resource, a friction between opposites. In the *Republic,* Plato talks about hierarchies between men and between men and gods. This latter story is the one from which Simone Weil takes 'metaxu'. She sharpens it into a dimensionless edge. She says that 'between' is a noun and its antonym: 'Every separation is a link': the between is a bridge. The world is a bridge. Somewhere on its other side is

II

A man is across from me in a window, two stories up. I forget what city I'm in. His ledge is lined by metal spikes; I suppose to keep the pigeons out. He is tan, only a sprinkle of hair on his chest. He smokes, talks to someone invisible. I cover most of my face with my left hand, look at him through the finger–splay. I assume he cannot see my irises. His privacy is a spectacle. I glimpse his bald spot. He turns, stares. This is irreversible.

III

I look at the artist's easel, his crown. From this angle he has a nice penumbra of hair. This wall between us, this canvas, is my blind–spot. When he shifts to understand a part of me, I can see his face. He finds my left eye with his right. Rattles a sigh. Taps his brush. I stare through this eclipse at our cross of colored tape on the wall and breathe: Red X Red X Red X

IV

When he paints my eyes and I stare through him what happens? Some photons bounce off him, enter my retina, turn cis–retinoic acid into trans–retinoic acid. He moves. I get used to his dark. The white lights of the eyes, says the great teacher Robert Henri, must be made with the wooden end of a brush, in one deft movement, sacrificing everything.

V

Cats walk over my feet in the final set. The timer beeps. I do not let him watch me dress. 'Now you draw me,' he says, sets the timer for another five. I zero in on the shadow beneath his wrinkled collar. He pauses, thinks. Chin on fist, eyes down, he offers up his bald spot.

VI

My supersensuous realm has chaos also. My God is a mystery only because we are not whole, not wholly employing what is ours. Dogs, they tell me, see in black and white. I told my dog this. He barked then scratched his ear with his left foot. If we could see to the ends of the universe, we could know where he is – or – how fast he is traveling. Never both. This last problem is not really a problem: it's just that by seeing god you move him, and he becomes something else.

VII

Tuesday. Woke up drained. Mosquito in the bedroom. He left his mark between my eyebrows. I dozed on the couch in the living room, trying to wait him out. I did not have the energy to reclaim my dreams, of which there were too many. I wrote only what I overheard at the end:

you cannot....if your project operates on enterprise
into which enterprise cannot step

VIII

Possible Interpretation: a dream retort to the Directeur des Études et de la Recherche de l'Institut de l'Histoire de l'Art in Paris who told me he could not help me with my project on artists and muses because it sounded 'at least in French, terribly elliptical'.

There

In the beginning, it was the mahogany V
in your upper lip that I loved,

the way you put your lethal white
teeth over the lower

when you finished a statement
as though you could

retract your words a little,
which only gave them emphasis,

like when you told me
we had *a kind of connection*

that seemed to you *unique*.
With silence surrounding it,

and your teeth biting its gravity back,
unique seemed something so grand

and barely utterable, similar
to how you once made *there* sound

when you told me *it just wasn't*,
rendering *there* a mistress

so light and immaterial
I could hardly grasp her—that is

get my hands around her throat.
What a thrifty muse you are

to cast out such words,
whole flocks of meaning,

only to round them up again,
licking and biting them back

behind the pearly gates of your palate
while I stand by recording

the ethereal promise that hovers
and hungers to be transcribed

in my imagination, indelibly,
and between us (thank heavens)

in disappearing ink.

Picasso's Last Muse

for Jacqueline Roque

In truth, I died long ago.

His hand slept on my ribs
while streetlight filtered in through blinds
splaying his face in sideways lines:
a staff of inimitable shadow.

I tried to lose myself there
in his genius, before he woke,
somewhere between his eye, his mind, his –

without thinking, I slipped

                    into the marrow of his hand.

CAROLINE BIRD

Born in 1986, Caroline Bird has received numerous awards for her work, including a major Eric Gregory Award in 2002. Collections include *Looking Through Letterboxes* (Carcanet, 2002), *Trouble Came to the Turnip* (Carcanet, 2006, shortlisted for the Dylan Thomas Prize), and *Watering Can* (Carcanet, 2009, achieved 'Poetry Book Society Recommendation.') She has read and discussed poems on BBC Radio, including Finelines, Woman's Hour and The Verb, and at venues including the Royal Festival Hall and the Hay, Cheltenham, Ledbury, Glasgow and Manchester Literary Festivals. She leads poetry workshops in schools, teaches at the Arvon Foundation, and in 2009 she was shortlisted for the Dylan Thomas Prize and was the youngest writer on the list at 22.

Corker

It's funny you should say that
because I was just about to make a voodoo replica
to whack your head on my erogenous zones.

It's funny you should ask
because I went to couples therapy to sex
a medicine ball on my own.

It's funny you should mention love
because I was just about to knife off my ear
so I could paint an engorged sunflower
that resembled a cut-off ear.

It's funny you should go there
because I was just about to roll a cigarette
ten miles long so I could smoke postcoitally
years and years after the mattress was gagged over
by touts at the tip.

It's funny you should laugh
because I was just about to jam my soul
into a wedding cake shaped like a volcano
with Turkish delight lava and intricately-dead locals
chiselled from icing.

It's funny you should wander off
because I was just about to lie prostrate in a bouncy castle
pretending to be a toddler tired of her parents
bickering about the price of UVF.

It's funny you already ate breakfast
because I was just about to inject identical amounts of butter
into each individual crumpet-hole using the needle
I found amongst the condoms in the strawberry fields.

It's funny you should stop my hand
because I was just about to gold our names on a public bench
in preparation for our simultaneous elderly deaths, in the bath,
wearing electric-blanket shower-caps and embracing knitted rabbits.

It's funny you should shrug
because I was just about to rip out my heart in the Odeon.

It's funny the dress-code is casual
because I was just about to assassinate Leonard Cohen
for spying on your naked shoulders.

It's funny you're hanging on for someone
because I was just about to dredge every atom
of tenderness from the rubber in my sneakers
that palpably trembles whenever I'm waiting
by a doorway, a phone, a computer or a carrier pigeon.

It's funny you should text
because I was just about to slice a line in the sand
with a samurai letter-opener to see if
you'd left me a message in the bowels of the beach.

It's funny you should end it here
because I was just about to write the most successful love poem
this world has ever known and circulate it around stiff
universities where, like a Mexican wave, every repressed
woman in itchy tights would suddenly leave their jobs,
their families, their memory-choked houses and kneel
outside your window crying 'if I could be wanted like you,
I'd believe in angels ...'

Joy Is Like a Hungry Pig

Joy is like a hungry pig because there's always
a trough of it and kids get it all over their noses
and their parents have to hose them down in the garden.

There is a rumour that if you get too much joy
on your clothes, you start to oink and your fingers
fuse into trotters but that's just the men and women upstairs

with the knives and forks, trying to keep us all
miserable. They don't want hungry pigs galumphing
joyfully around their bowling alleys of lifelessness:

who knows, antique teashops might hoist themselves up
from their soil and concrete foundations and start marching
into Charing Cross, whistling with their kettles, 'I'm young!

I'm young! I'm young!' resulting in HUNGRY PIG
pandemonium, then (and think on this) a warm muddy glob
might land on the chin of someone who rejected you

and, before you know it, mad crazy joy is lathered up
the walls like excrement and you are the only one clean,
standing in a dry field with an empty wheelbarrow.

Shall I Compare Thee

Through the streets of damp brick, I came forth
with an engagement ring strapped to my leg
in a harsh leather pouch, and my chin
was a still-life and my mascara was waterproof
and I couldn't have stopped it
with an IRA surprise party.
I came to a door. The door was bolted
with string. There was a ramp for wheelchairs
your ex-lover put in, after the accident.
I kneecapped myself with spontaneous love
I'd been planning for months in my cell
of a bedroom where trays were left out,
muffins and tea, by my nervous relations
who suspect you of larceny. But I was alive
in a tangential way, one knee in a rain-puddle
on your front porch. At least, I think it was you.
The ring shook in my hand like a renegade
dew-drop destined for higher things
and you said 'NO,' which I figured was wise.
Your frown hit my gut like a battered mars bar
but, unembarrassed, I tried next door:
the doorbell arpeggioed like an elderly lush,
the security-light was as weak as chat,
but they said 'YES' and we've been tight
as cheap elastic bands around the ponytails of children
these past years of happiness.

Grand Finale

What starts in a jazz club must end in a candle shop.
Recently, I've been broken hearted in John Lewis,
picking up plain white mugs and staring into them.
Just standing in the kitchen section of John Lewis,
staring into the bottom of a plain white mug.
Like a thin person watching their weight, I revere my idle duty.
What starts in a plush hotel must end on a dry stone wall.
You are shopping casually for candles.
You choose lemon-scented with a swirl trapped in it
while I think of restaurants and what starts in restaurants.
What if I punched out my lighter and lit the wick
before you'd paid for it?
Then you'd be a thief with a peck of stolen light.
What starts in a husky voice must end with an email.
I smoke on this dry stone wall and wait for the saxophones.

The One

I met the person of my dreams: dream voice,
dream body, dream pictures rising from dream cranium.
I said 'look, dreams are for sleeping people
You must be hideously lost, this isn't your realm.'
It mocked me for using the word 'realm.'
'Line-drawers like you,' it said, 'don't know the meaning
of the word "realm," I have a realm in my elastoplasts,
I have a realm in my hand as it reaches for the parking meter,
there isn't a realm without dreams.' 'There is,' I said,
'I'm getting married, I shouldn't be convorting with dreams.'
'Convorting?' it said, 'you don't know the meaning
of the word, I convort whilst eating an apple, my breathing
is a form of convorting.' To test its routine, I flicked
an egg in the air, bit in mid-flight, spat yolk and said
'Love to me is like a deep sorrow.'

'Sorrow!?' it screamed, 'sorrow?!
I could show you a place where little girls like you
snot into their computer keyboards with unrelenting
tears like a botched operation squirting from their face
in scissors of spit.' 'Sometimes,' I said, 'I get so lonely,
I watch pornography in my room and drink vodka
from a lamp-shade with the hole selotaped over.'
'Don't talk to me about loneliness,' the dream retorted,
'I could show you a block of ice straining to open arms
it doesn't have, unmelting on a warm, finger-marked bed
unable to think of anything but empty fridges.'

'What about despair?' I said. 'Oh, I can offload a crate
of despair in half an hour,' it said, 'given the right van
with an attractive logo.' 'I've thought of suicide!' I yelled,
getting into the spirit. 'You're a baby,' it said
between violent guffaws, 'you don't know jack about the jaded
awful feeling of smashing the only jam-jar that contained
the best of your oxygen, the best of your love-making,

tumble-dryers butchering boxer-shorts, and your lover
crying naked, praying for a time-machine!'

I'd never met a damaged dream before: they'd always been
relatively upbeat, ribbons waving on a stick, Tina Turner singing
'Eye of the Tiger' on tape. Or else, they were nightmares.
This definitely wasn't a nightmare. It was dream. A good dream.
A brilliant dream. So what if my tear-ducts were bleeding?

After 'Passion.' 'Passion?!' and 'Dishonour.' 'Dishonour?'
we reached a standstill. 'Shall we go back to yours?' I said.
'I've given you the wrong impression,' it said, wincing,
'How so?' I said, unbuckling my belt. 'You think I'm *your* dream,'
it said, 'I don't belong to anyone, I'm self-employed, I steal
brain-cells from various sources to sell on Ebay. I'm joking.
Put your trousers back on.' By this time, I'd fallen in love.
'Show me the places where the acorns slit their wrists
to let the bud out,' I garbled, pretentiously. 'I could show
you the *meaning* of love,' the dream boasted,
'give me a spare afternoon and a couple of second-hand books
but things are pretty hectic until September
and you, my adorable talented dreamer,
need to go beddy-byes.'

Public Detectives

I've been listening to your day through the wall
of a whole city. Sometimes the wires cross and I listen
to an old Taiwanese woman muttering to her cats.
I've been eavesdropping on your progress
with a glass tumbler pressed to a tube map.
I've been conferring, finally, with other reluctant troubadours:
they've sent single red roses to half the population
and still no girlish stammer from those macho dialing tones.
It's as if no one's listening except us.

You've been watching my day through the keyhole
of a scientific discovery. Sometimes the light flips and
you watch a dying puppy staring longingly at a sausage.
You've been measuring our time apart in guilty shrugs
when silent crowds mention me. You've been conferring,
finally, with the other burdened troubadours:
they've sent boxes of ice to half the population
and still no macho dialing tones from those girlish stammers.
It's as if no one's listening except us.

What Shall We Do with Your Subconscious?

I'm tired of watching the riots and knowing
which young boys will be bodies by sundown.
I saw the bomb growing in the womb. I saw
you run and run and run while you kissed me.

I'm tired of playing cards with money that's
already gone and the drugs kicking in during
an exam I'm bound to pass and not just pass
but take charge of. I was and am a golden girl

in the past tense of the present tense, the drink
will lose your mind and there's no such thing
as a pre-emptive strike: can't you see the ash
falling on your yellow omelettes? It's a kind

of gift, they say, but callings are supposed to
call you somewhere. I'm tired of schoolyards
chequered with prepubescent bankers who'll
attempt to hang themselves once. This plane

has many dangling oxygen masks like a tree,
like a crashing tree. Do you understand me?
I saw prostitutes in wheelchairs by the pool
but this city won't burn, it will refuse to burn

for the sake of occasional happiness. Blimps.
Pistachios. Holding hands. I cannot foresee
you holding my hand yet I hear the evening
cockerel and I'm tired of the singing graves.

Three Strikes

I lost one and then I lost the other.
I lost one to keep the other
but the other didn't want to be kept,
not like that, not as an accidental
second catch of the baseball match
with your palm outstretched to feel for rain.
The first didn't want to be lost
or kept, it was tricky. Dabbles of light
came through my open window and lay
across my empty bed. I lost one
and when you lose one, a little voice says, 'Hey
why not lose the other?' This is how
it becomes a streak. Did I say I lost two?
I lost three. Now I'm really boasting.
I lost one to keep the other two.
I say 'lost.' One was eaten by time.
One was lost before the curtain came up.
One I plan to find on this road.
'It took me three to know the virtue of one,'
is what I tell the barman. But I was lost
in three places. Lost once at a family Christmas,
lost twice at the dawn of my enlightenment,
lost three times by the red alarm clock
in the cupboard under the stairs of my ribs –
call it my ticker. Hang on, that makes six.
And the first loss always counts for ten.

CARMEN BUGAN

Born in 1970 in Romania, Carmen Bugan was a Creative Arts Fellow in Literature at Wolfson College, Oxford (2005-2009) and a Hawthornden Fellow (2004). She has received an Arts Council of England grant. Her publications include a collection of poems, *Crossing the Carpathians* (Oxford*Poets*/Carcanet, 2004), and poetry and prose in *Harvard Review, PN Review, Tabla Book of New Verse, Forward Book of Poetry, Penguin's Poems for Life,* the *Times Literary Supplement,* and *Modern Poetry in Translation.* Educated at the University of Michigan and Balliol College, Oxford, with a doctorate in Irish poetry, she lives near Geneva, Switzerland, with her husband and son. (Photo courtesy of Alessandro Tricoli.)

The House of Straw

in memory of my grandparents

[This poem describes *grijirea*, a ritual practised around the villages in the Moldavian region of Romania to prepare people for the afterlife.]

"In this world the house will be yours
But in the afterlife it shall be mine."
So, when they were old, they joined
In the ritual of caring for the band
Of gypsies coming through the village,
Looking after parents left by children
At empty hearths. What you give away
Stays with you in eternity,
For heaven or hell will be received
In a familiar bed, at a table you know.

Each built a separate room in the garden;
Walls and floor of new straw rugs.
A bed with a hay mattress draped in cotton,
White pillows, change of clothes,
Soft slippers to walk around the sky,
A table with chairs, a flower tapestry,
A pail filled with water from our well.
For work, each gave away bags of rice
Which needed separating grain by grain,
Beans, a sack of un-sifted wheat,
Corn in a wicker basket, and two hens
To lay eggs around the house.
All other time in heaven is leisurely, they said.

*

And then, the afterlife meal:
Onions, rice, fresh tomatoes were sweated
In sunflower oil, then added to minced meat,
Flavored with parsley and dill, some salt,

Ground pepper, an egg for binding up the mixture,
All wrapped in vine leaves stung in brine
And put to simmer all day long.
Grandmother hovered over polenta
With the wooden spoon, while buttermilk,
Aged in earthen jugs, was ready to be poured.

*

When the poor in this life were called
To receive the roofless houses of straw
Candles were lit to link the living day
To the other world with the cord of light;
I watched all those hands uniting
On stems of wax held at thresholds,
I saw love eternal, burning at open doors.
Then in his room, my grandfather brought
A flask of wine, set it on the table, and cried.

Making Wine

I

All August we washed oak barrels
Fitted them with shiny hoops
Rolled them slowly to our well,
Filled each one to the brim, leaving
The water to swell the staves.

II

When the frost fell, her elbows
White with flour, sank in dough,
Round loaves baked in our clay oven,
Sheep cheese was on the table
Unwrapped from its cloth.

It was always early morning.
Blind with sleep I received
The water she poured on my hands
From the tin cup; a little chill
Came through the opened door.

Now I hear grinding of hooves,
Yoking creaks, horses breathing,
Slow rolling of wheels
On the road to the vineyard, I see
The seam of trees around our field.

III

We each took a row: grapes hung
Heavy with sweetness, weighty, strange
With cold skin, ripeness, fragrance:

I crushed them between my palms
To show my part in harvest.

Those were long days filled with sun
Grapes in baskets, naps under oaks,
Grandparents' musings over tannin
In the wine ...

IV

The pressing always began
With grandmother offering food
And grandfather pouring old wine
To family and neighbors, until
Red in the cheeks, we washed our feet
And went dancing in the barrel.

She in a flowery dress and
Him wearing a black suit ...
I saw her return underground,
Keened the best I knew
But last time I spoke with him
He sat waiting in the quiet yard.

V

The priest smiles as I take a mouthful
Of wine from the bottle he brought
As a wedding gift: 'It's from your fields'
He says. I hear the clambering noise
Of time which never seemed to end
It ended, and now begins again.

Making the Hay Mattress

The best part of all that was dancing:
In August, at the summer cleaning
She threw away mattresses and pillows

Stripping our bed to an idea on the empty floor,
Where, with hammer and nails she reinforced
Wobbly corners of the wooden frame.

Then in a new white case we stuffed fresh hay;
After she sealed it, she summoned us to dance
The *hora* on top to even out the surface

Soften flowers, herbs and grass.
Barefoot, we took lessons on the mattress
Stomped our feet, clapped our hands, laughed.

So it was that till the day she died,
We danced in August and slept on flowers at night.

Harvesting Walnuts

Early in October, when our walnut tree
Began to drop a nut here, one there,
First letting go of the green husks,
With a *pluck* and a *plump* then a *thump,*

Grandfather carved sticks, thick as our arms;
We climbed the tree to knock down the wallnuts:
From between leaves a bitter smell of iodine
Fell. Back on the ground we sat in a circle

Holding round stones in yellow-stained hands,
We cracked walnuts, built leaf castles
Guarded by turtle armies made of husks
And shells, and we learned the colour bitter-green.

Acciecati dalla meraviglia

['Blind with wonder']

Unchanged, the white curtain in the marble hall
Still half-hanging from the fallen rail

A stack of maps the child couldn't reach that first night,
Still on the gray countertop, at the head of the stairs,

The same noise from cheap shops, where they sold
Skirts and trinkets to us refugees emerging, wide-eyed

From the end of all trail-tracks at Roma Termini, and first
Memory of self with one suitcase, making a right turn

Out of the station. Then, finding, as the blind does,
Whispers counting time in the ventricles

Of Santa Maria Maggiore, on each side of the nave,
From confession box to confession box.

To honor the year when we were blinded by wonder here
I walk through the same streets, revisit ancient ruins,

In a story beginning in the year one hundred and six with Trojan
I, blood of Dacian beekeeper or weapon-clad conqueror, flow
 inside Rome,

Shivering in the sun, not knowing what I am, as voices
From across two thousand years collect in my flesh.

The Names of Things

Sunlight in a water bowl on the doorstep
Then on a pond far from home: *soarele*.

Fire in the terracotta hearth, then
In a pit, outside a tent, thousands of miles away: *focul*.

My Black Sea lulling the shore, then dreams
Of sea waking the cheeks with stinging salt: *marea*.

Air encircling the grapes outside the window,
Then gliding with a parachute above a heron: *aerul*.

Soil exhaling after rain through gaps between cherry leaves.
Then crying dirty tears from roots of a fallen birch: *pamintul*.

Soarele, focul, marea, aerul, pamintul:
There or here – speaking, whispering, calling.

The Rook

The whole month of June I saw
How with broken claw and wings,
It called to the forest, refused strawberries,
Kept towards the canopy of trees.

Then the fifth Sunday came,
We lifted the cage bidding it farewell.
Tar-black, it flapped quickly, flew
In a circle as if to take off, then fell.

*

He said he stood outside the gates
Until they told him to take the first train.
There, in that station where convicts
Come and go, he cried, a free man.

Mating Swans

She stood still in the centre of the lake,
Head high, raised tail, white calligraphy,

He made a clock on the face of the water
Arresting the sun, her gaze and the reeds;

From the tongue of twelve o'clock he
Bowed before her as a question mark

And she answered with her own bow,
A question, before him: turn following

Turn. When he mounted her
I called you and we blushed together

Through their dance of coiling necks,
Kissing beaks, and beating wings.

At the end two questions faced each other
Raising a heart on the face of the water.

We too, that morning, bowed
And drew on our blue cotton sheets.

KATE CLANCHY

Kate Clanchy's three collections of poetry, *Slattern*, *Samarkand*, and *Newborn* (Picador) have brought her several literary awards, including the Somerset Maugham, Saltire, and Forward Prizes. Her poems are widely anthologised and a selection have been translated into Italian as *Neonato* (Medusa, 2008). Since beginning to write prose, she has won the Writers' Guild Award for Best Book of 2009 for *Antigona and Me*, a memoir, and the 2009 National Short Story Award for 'The Not-Dead and the Saved.' She lives in Oxford with her family. (Photo courtesy of Macmillan Publishers Ltd.)

Love

I hadn't met his kind before.
His misericord face – really
like a joke on his father – blurred
as if from years of polish;
his hands like curled dry leaves;

the profligate heat he gave
out, gave out, his shallow,
careful breaths: I thought
his filaments would blow,
I thought he was an emperor,

dying on silk cushions.
I didn't know how to keep
him wrapped, I didn't know
how to give him suck, I had
no idea about him. At night

I tried to remember the feel
of his head on my neck, the skull
small as a cat's, the soft spot
hot as a smelted coin,
and the hair, the down, fine

as the innermost, vellum layer
of some rare snowcreature's
aureole of fur, if you could meet
such a beast, if you could
get so near. I started there.

Infant

In your frowning, fugitive days, small love,
your coracled, ecstatic nights,
possessed or at peace, hands clenched
on an unseen rope, or raised in blessing
like the Pope, as your white etched feet
tread sooty roofs of canal tunnels
or lie released, stretched north in sleep –

you seem to me an early saint, a Celt,
eyes fixed on a celestial light, patiently
setting the sextant straight
to follow your godsent map, now
braced against a baffling gale, now
becalmed, fingers barely sculling
through warm muddy tides.

Soon, you will make your way out
of this estuary country, leave
the low farms and fog banks, tack through
the brackish channels and long
reed-clogged rivulets, reach
the last turn, the salt air and river mouth,
the wide grey sea beyond it.

When You Cried

I sat and mourned, let you
thrash on my lap like a choking fish.
The way your soft spine
chain-linked, grew strong!

It was as if you were a salmon
and our arms were nets, as if
you were searching upstream, upstream,
for the dark pool

you came from, for your
proper ground. I thought
you'd seen through us,
that you knew this wasn't home.

Rejoice in the Lamb

At night, in your shift, fine hair upright,
you are my tiny Bedlamite,
admonishing the laughing crowd
with your pale, magisterial hands,
or roaring out like poor Kit Smart
how blessed, electric, all things are.

The Burden

I'd never have thought that this would be me,
content to tote the baby homewards
answering, rook-like, his hoarse calls,
counting the haws on the bare claw branches,
the rose hips shining like blood.

And you'd be the one at the gate left staring
at the cloud-shadows etched on the copper water,
the flooded fields we couldn't cross.
That I'd let a hundred yards stretch between us.
How bright this thin, bisected moon.

Aneurysm

When my father heard his friend
was dead, we sat a while and talked
of traffic: how cars clog
each by-way now, every road
you think you know. We were quiet,
and I lit the lamp. I thought

I could hear the cars outside,
bashing, lowing, rank on rank.
There'd been a crash, my father said,
and his friend had walked out,
shaken, saved. It was hours
before the blood-clot got him.

I held my baby on my lap. It was
dark, it was the winter solstice.
We said there is no such thing
as the right route or a clear passage
no matter where you start,
or how you plan it.

Plain Work

We should knit, Joanna,
or tat, however that is done.
These winter afternoons -
we should drop wood eggs
down socks, or hold
long knotted wefts between us.

We should have stuff
to show for this: for the days
we've sat together, waiting
for our babies to get over
a tooth, a want, a croupy fever;
to get an hour older.

Yards of it by now – enough
to fill this room, surround us.
Great rolls of random rainbow
cloth, twisted, lumpen, fine,
the bright wool stitched in,
stitched in, line by line.

Ararat

Winter of floods – winter of broken banks
and radio warnings and me running
down the road with the pushchair screaming
and a cloud helicoptering low behind me.

Remember even the genteel Cherwell
bursting, the Isis brimming, swelling under
its muddy meniscus like a body rolling
in sleep in a blanket? The times you came home

to find the armchairs floating, the carpet
a quicksand, the tables at unprecedented levels,
the baby awash in his Moses basket and me
bailing madly as he rose to the ceiling?

Yet here we all are, no worse than muddy, and look –
the hills emerging, exactly the same, casual as knees.

Storm

So, here
at the height
of this summer
of wrong, in this wrong
hour of this most wrong day
in the heart of the week which went
awry, now while the rain washes
the window free of every
roof we know, of every
tree, you and I, small
one, have come
to an impasse.

You're red,
half-dressed, push-
ing our car up the hill
of the chair. I'm white, flatout
in a field of trousers, listening
to the wind – which is your own twin,
darling – howl for its place, for
its proper season, and bash
our doors and walls
with its enormous
kitchen roll tube
trumpet.

The Other Woman

I am running to meet her,
now, the girl who lives on her own,
who has in her hand the key to her own
hallway, her own bare polished stair, who
is clacking down it now, in kitten heels, swearing,
who is marching over envelopes marked with a single name,
who is late, can be late, sleep late, forget things,
who tonight has forgotten hat, gloves and
umbrella, and is running not caring
through the luminous rain.
What shall we say?

Shall I slip off
my coat and order cold wine
and watch myself sip it through
the long row of optics, arching my back
on the velvet banquette? And pick up the wit,
the moue of the mouth as we pass jokes like olives?
And say the right thing and stand up for my round,
tapping the bar with a rolled-up twenty,
tipsy, self-conscious, a girl,
a vessel of secrets, so
carefully held in?

Or down just one glass
and see stars and the whole
room go smeary, have nothing to say
and say all the same – apropos of nothing,
in the middle of everything – *You don't understand.*
What happens is someone slips from your side, someone
full-sized. Will she yawn, get her bag, start tucking
her fags in when I get out his photo,
say *Look, look how he's grown,*
all by himself, he has grown
to the size of my life?

CONSTANTINE CONTOGENIS

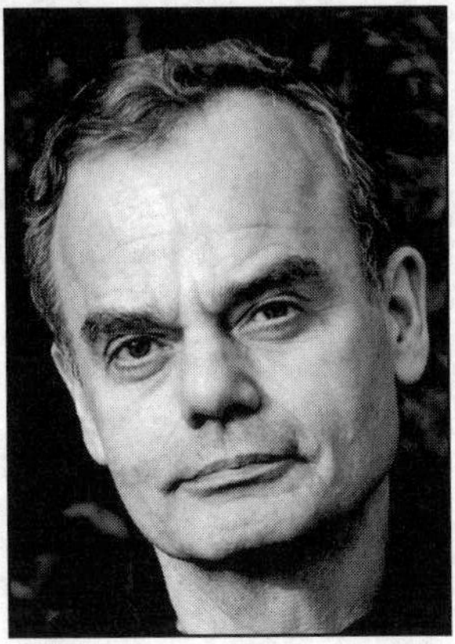

Constantine Contogenis's poetry collection *Ikaros* (Word Press, 2004) received First Prize "Open Voice Poetry Award" from Writer's Voice. He is co-translator of *Songs of the Kisaeng: Courtesan Poetry of the Last Korean Dynasty* (BOA Editions, 1997), and was poet-in-residence (2000-2001), Purchase College, State University of New York. His work has appeared in *Paris Review, Literary Imagination, TriQuarterly, Chicago Review, Cimarron Review, Asian Pacific American Journal, MacGuffin, Marlboro Review, Meridian Anthology of Contemporary Poetry, Poetry East, New Orleans Review, NY Quarterly, Speakeasy, Worcester Review, Grand Street, South Carolina Review,* and *Zone 3,* and has been featured on Verse Daily and on the Poetry Society of America's Poetry in Motion® for public buses and trains. (Photo courtesy of Lee Wexler.)

There Are No Ploughs on Ikaria

Since Brueghel was always right
about suffering, notice
how he gets the island wrong:
a few quick generations

split up fields to fierce gardens.
A few intolerant States
exile resisters, whom no
furrows distract from this sea.

Notice that Auden vouches
for the painting and gets it
wrong. Nothing turns away. No
man hears the cry and does not

turn. No ship sees a falling
boy and calmly does not turn.
No torturer of talent
would take work in such a place.

Looking Like It

You get the look from old movies: Mifune
warns that his sword will hurt; Belmondo
French-inhales after; and the jig up,
Milland serves them drinks. Moreau taking

Jules and Jim down with her ... But Truffaut's
slow motion suicides make you wonder
what their looks are like when the car hits
and the water begins to take them down.

Pain you can't wait to end makes you wait
real time. Pull the noose of a sweater
over your head. Reach for your gun
– your draw's quick as his; push the trigger

– now it's all up to your aim. Cards speak
at the showdown – don't cry, don't laugh.
Show the poker-facing table what means
so much, you won't give its meaning a sign.

Zeno's Arrow

I sail when I can, which is not an hour a week
but a day a year. It's plenty, really.
The days come quickly, and most every year
I make way against the wind. The masthead
tenses, sketches lines as high as I can see
but never flies. The boat keeps to water,
comes about to face the wind.

Just because I return to where I leave
doesn't mean I contradict the wind.
I don't believe it takes offense. We both obey
arbitrary laws. When tacking we try
to keep the sail between us but – each time
it seems unnatural – the wind
can't help but come over to my side.

The God's Final Words To Antony

In the middle of the night, a sudden
noise from a passing crowd you cannot see,
then their music, ecstatic, their shouts
– no, don't, your luck is now over,
the works of your life are mistakes,
your plans are lies, so grief means little.
Say goodbye to her as if you always knew
the reason for your courage, say it as she goes away.
Whatever happens, don't demean yourself with hopes,
don't start fooling yourself by claiming
it was a dream, so your ears were not hearing.
As if your courage was in knowing this would come,
which is why you were given this kind of city,
walk to the window, walk steadily,
listen with care and with feeling, no,
without the requests, the denials of a coward,
this, here is your final pleasure, listen
to that music, those instruments, the procession,
now, say goodbye, to Alexandria, the city you are losing.

– a wrenched translation
from the Greek of C.P. Cavafy

The Trick

You discover there's no trick to it;
you happen on it either way.
Getting older ought to change it
– and it does no longer come in color.
Those looks, too, from those who saw you
swim to the ship and climb aboard
stop. But if you don't pay much mind,
it floats back in sight, making way,
taking straight course. And you still wish
– it just happens – for the same time
to tell if it approached
or chugged the other way.

Ikaros

Before he hit, another
breathing creature timed its leap
to kiss him hard, break his skin,
teeth, nose, but blasted its own breath

to his brain, waking a taste
of salt, the knowledge of
entering the sea as he did
and last thoughts of dolphin.

Before falling, unable
to read clouds, he baited air
with feathers and sweat, was caught
by a thermal: across his

shoulders an octopus of air
sucked at the hairs of his arms,
until islands receded,
and he knew he was of age.

Before losing sight of his
father, he had stopped looking,
having no more amazement
for making, for how the man

with wings continued to shape
the air, as he let it prove
what slant of extended wings
soared, dived, and kept him in air.

Before escape, he was shamed
by flapping his arms like a
bird, by the pains, the muscles
growing inside chest and neck,

by his father's practiced change
of direction between glides,
making separate things part of
himself, himself part of things.

Before the wings were ready,
Daedalos taught him to make
glues from boiled hooves, test them
with honeycombs, and give names

to the ones stone seals could mark
but wheels could not pull apart.
With a tanning knife, he cut
the signets out of the wax.

Before their imprisonment,
he watched as his father made
oak platforms, bronze hinges, and
Egyptian ropes cease to be

metal, wood, fiber. When he
tried to catch the changes in-
to catapult or light spear,
he became too slow or quick.

Before sanctioned entry to
his father's workshop, he sought
sad girls to question, sick men
to watch die. He introduced

himself to weeping women,
was aroused to ask the names
of their loved dead. Excited,
their answers to him were signs.

Before there was a workbench,
he kept eyes to the wind until
he blinked or cried. He built walls
with holes facing the strongest

winds, wedged thin crystals, and looked
into the heart of the lung,
back at the eye, heard last breaths,
saw nothing there to be seen.

Before his father told him
the idea of windows, he
loved both sides of walls, locusts
leaving carapaces, ewes

licking newborns free of last
membranes, fish breaching the first
time, eggshells pushed in on wet
feathers, the dead in his life.

Ignatios's Gravestone

In here I'm not the Cleon who liked to be told
– in Alexandria (where it's hard to impress) –
about my splendid houses, and their grounds,
about the horses and carriages I owned,
about the jewels and the silks that I wore.
I tell you: I am not that Cleon –
let his 28 years be extinguished!
I'm the Ignatios, sacred reader, it took me that long
to know – but so I won ten months of happiness
through the quiet and certainties of Christ.

– a wrenched translation
from the Greek of C.P. Cavafy

Elocution

Long scratch on the river water ooze
that arcs so near straight it claims a center
so far fetched that the earth could be drawn to
must mean tidal currents reach upstream

cracking the surface, slowing the flow down.
Here's that ideal spot for learning river,
drinking the sound from the front to the back of the mouth,
you know, for beating mountain streams to the bay

a while. For watching the river unflow
a benchy bench would be self-evident,
the word's falling sound for a belle and beau,
below, river past them, above, the river past.

GREG DELANTY

Greg Delanty was born in Cork City, Ireland, and now teaches at Saint Michael's College, Vermont. He has received many awards, most recently a Guggenheim for poetry. The magazine *Agenda* devoted a recent issue to his 50th birthday. The National Library of Ireland acquired his papers up to 2012. He is Vice President of the Association of Literary Scholars, Critics, and Writers, and will become President of this Association in October 2010. He is presently editing *The Word-Exchange: Anglo-Saxon Poems in Translation,* forthcoming from W.W. Norton. The poems featured here are from his *Collected Poems 1986-2006* (Oxford*Poets*/Carcanet Press, 2007) and his next book of poems *The Greek Anthology, Book XVII.* (Photo courtesy of Brian MacDonald, Saint Michael's College.)

To My Mother, Eileen

I'm threading the eye
of the needle for you again. That is
my specially appointed task, my
gift that you gave me. Ma, watch me slip this
camel of words through. Yes,
rich we are still even if your needlework
has long since gone with the rag-and-bone man
and Da never came home one day, our Dan.
Work Work Work. Lose yourself in work.
That's what he'd say.
Okay okay.
Ma, listen, I can hear the sticks of our fire spit
like corn turning into popcorn
with the brown insides of rotten teeth. We sit
in our old Slieve Mish house. Norman is just born.
He's in the pen.
I raise the needle to the light and lick the thread
to stiffen the limp words. I
peer through the eye, focus, put everything out of my head.
I shut my right eye and thread.
I'm important now, a likely lad, instead
of the amadán at Dread School. I have the eye
haven't I, the knack?
I'm Prince Threader. I missed it that try.
Concentrate. Concentrate. Enough yaketty yak.
There, there, Ma, look, here's the threaded needle back.

Aceldama

And Judas cast down the pieces of silver in the temple, and departed. And the chief priests and elders took counsel, and bought with the pieces of silver the potter's field, to bury strangers in. Wherefore that field was called, The Field of Blood, unto this day.

– Matthew 27:5-8

We drove down what seemed the curve
of the earth, sandwiched in our Ford Anglia.
We were happy as the colors of our beachball,
a careless car full of mirth and singalong songs,
songs that were mostly as sappy
as the soppy tomato sandwiches sprinkled with sand,
which is why they're called sandwiches our father said,
sandwiched himself now in the ground between his mother
and ours. What's the meaning of dead?
Which one of us children asked that as we passed
the spot with the lit steel cross on Carr's Hill,
putting the kibosh on the next song,
our mother about to break into *Beautiful City*?
She crossed herself, saying that's the place they bury
those whose lives somehow went wrong, betrayed
in one way or other, without a song to their names,
or a name, everyone together
and alone without a headstone.
The crepuscular loneliness of the field
shrouded our bright time. Our world,
the city below, shimmered like the silver pieces
scattered on the dark floor of the temple.

The Compositor

Perhaps it's the smell of printing ink
sets me off out of memory's jumbled font
or maybe it's printer's lingo
as he relates how phrases came about.

How for instance *mind your p's and q's*
has as much to do with pints & quarts
and the printer's renown for drink
as it has with those descenders.

But I don't say anything about
how I discovered where *widows & orphans*
and *out of sorts* came from the day my father
unnoticed and unexpectedly set *30*

on the bottom of his compositor's page
and left me mystified about the origins
of that end, how to measure a line gauge
and how, since he was first to go,

he slowly and without a word
turned from himself into everyone
as we turn into that last zero
before finally passing on to the stoneman.

The Phone Bird

For days I've stayed within range of the phone,
        tethered to my need the way the phone is tethered
                to itself. Some days I listen so hard
                        I'm sure I hear it ring.
When anyone calls, they're dumbstruck
        as my shaky greeting turns to despondency.
I admit that if you rang there'd be times
        you'd get an earful for not ringing.
                You know how I brood, turned in
on myself, willing the snake-coiled phone to ring,
        the handset clamped like devouring jaws on the rest.
Now the phone's a sleeping bird with its head tucked
        back in its wing. If you call,
I'll unfurl its neck and tenderly, tenderly I'll sing.

The Sea Horse Family

The sea horse is a question-mark in the ark of the ocean
that's carried it without question all this way.
Mythical as a unicorn, and even less believable
with its dragon head, its body a legless horse
perpetually rearing, its monkey tail
anchoring it to sea grass, sponge or coral,
but, my mate,
no stranger than who you are to yourself,
feeling large as a whale and small as a human.
Today I'd have us become sea horses, and I,
being the male, would be the one in the family way.
I'd lug our hippocampus, our *capall mara*, our shy sea pony,
our question-mark anchored in you,
unquestionably unfurling its self day by tidal day.

The Alien

I'm back again scrutinizing the Milky Way
        of your ultrasound, scanning the dark
                matter, the nothingness, that now the heads say
        is chockablock with quarks & squarks,
gravitons & gravitini, photons & photinos. Our sprout,

who art there inside the spacecraft
        of your ma, the time capsule of this printout,
                hurling & whirling towards us, it's all daft
        on this earth. Our alien who art in the heavens,
our Martian, our little green man, we're anxious

to make contact, to ask questions
        about the heavendom you hail from, to discuss
                the whole shebang of the beginning & end,
        the pre-big bang untime before you forget the why
and lie of thy first place. And, our friend,

to say Welcome, that we mean no harm, we'd die
        for you even, that we pray you're not here
                to subdue us, that we'd put away
        our ray guns, missiles, attitude and share
our world with you, little big head, if only you stay.

Four Poems from *The Greek Anthology, Book XVII*

Fall Out

Today I read a poet's elegy for his friend
        written forty years after he passed away.
It hurt me to read, how friendship still shone,
        a paradigm of friendlove, the jewel
in the crown of life. And I thought of you,
        and wished I was that poet, and you had died
in the good old days, and it was I wrote that poem
        to you, my friend, my sometime friend.

– Gregory of Corkus

Terminal

And so, Tithonus, you're hooked
        to ventilator, catheter or canula; gagging down
another pill, unable to fend for yourself, praying
        to be released from the drip
as malignant cells metastasize,
        make nothing of you.
Dawn even abandons you
        in the snug-as-a-coffin terminal room.
Nurses turn you over, change your diaper.
        You're unable to recall your own name,
remember you can't remember; eternally
        aware dementia erases the spool.
The gods, as usual, show no pity.

– *Honestmedon*

Parents

What do any of us know about our parents,
    separate or together? My mother kept the house
in order, prepared food, wore the *epinetron* smooth
    rolling the threads, the skeins of daily love.
She wove our clothes, played knucklebones, snakes & ladders,
    lined up with other women at the well,
walked home balancing the vase on her head
    as she balanced our family, the *oikos*.
Like most parents she hid her care, sadness, the arguments
    with my father heading off on another odyssey.
Da played dead when I stabbed him, let me
    wear his helmet; turned into a tickle monster.
Ma scolded him for exciting me before bed.
    I suppose they were like most parents. What do I know?
I had no others. They were as mysterious as the night sky,
    the Islands of the Blest, the sea, Hades, the god
hidden within the darkness of the forbidden inner temple.

– *Danichorus*
Fragment from the lost poem Telemachus

The Traveler's Grace

Nothing like landing in a foreign city
early morning. Preferably in weekday hubbub.
Everyone going about their business, lost in themselves,
not a thought of how alien, foreign, strange their lives are.
How abnormal to think it normal to find ourselves
on a spinning ball speeding around a star
at thousands of miles per hour from who knows where
to who knows where. How outlandish.
I'm one of the sacred dead,
released from the underworld
of the mundane, the banal. Behold the normal.

– *Gregory of Corkus*

JANE DRAYCOTT

Jane Draycott's most recent collection, *Over* (Oxford*Poets*), was nominated for the 2009 T.S. Eliot Prize. Named one of the Poetry Book Society's '*Next Generation*' poets in 2004, she is Senior Tutor on Oxford University's MSt in Creative Writing, and lectures on postgraduate writing programmes at Lancaster University. Collections include *No Theatre* and *Prince Rupert's Drop* (both shortlisted for the Forward Prize for Poetry) and *The Night Tree,* a PBS Recommendation 2004. Her translation of the medieval dream-vision *Pearl*, a Stephen Spender Prize-winner in 2008, is due from Oxford*Poets* in 2011. Poems appear courtesy Oxford*Poets*/Carcanet, Two Rivers Press, *Modern Poetry in Translation,* and *Poetry London.* (Photo courtesy of Ian MacDonald.)

Blue

Some thought they heard *flight,* others
that *fight* was the syllable uttered
on the floor of the forest, the young man
far from home, unable to tell us even his name.

All afternoon those among us convinced
they knew the root of a word when they saw it
argued the toss between *agony* and *ecstasy*

the green of his jacket the whole while dividing,
bursting towards the light, his mouthful of soot
spat upward in a fountain of feathers or leaves.

Night fell. We bent to the bones, hoping to hear
like the Bible translated against all laws
some sounds we might more easily swallow.
Kneeling, we listened.

Westernays

for Bernard

is when your car ends facing backwards
    on the wrong side of the road

when the wind beats your umbrella
    till its insides all hang out

when the water takes your little boat
    and spins it like a plate.

It's like a song reversed, a church
    constructed widershins

to face the falling sun, the day
    next week or sometime soon

you'll take a truth and twist it,
    turn a child to face the wall

or force a man stark naked
    to get down and lick the floor.

It's the dream which has you driving
    down exactly the wrong street

as you race to reach your boat
    before it sails.

It's the wind along the western quay,
    the voices in its throat

the seaman on the closing doors,
    the words you hear him shout

I'll wait. I'll wait all night
if need be. I can wait.

Milestone

At this milestone rest after all that
racing about torch-leaves
down on the ground for you
the small red boats the empty public road.

By this milestone wait your bare feet
on the stone's stone your face tipped up
to catch a bit of sun your resting heart
dissolving even in simple rainwater.

Fare thee well our hearts like brooches
hung from the trees. How far can you be?

Prospect

Anyone who wanted to could leave, could gather
    shivering on the south side of the river,
labelled and provided for with socks and sweaters
    and a little cash. We walked across the water
in our thousands and left behind for ever
    all that was great: the monuments and sewers,
cathedrals, theatres, mothers, lovers, brothers
    as the flames licked at the city's raging heart.

Faced with the prospect of living forever,
    we headed for the country lanes together,
imagining the *parties de campagne* among the clover
    and the stories each would tell the others
on the way. We had left behind for ever
    all that we had loved. It was a start.

Papa

The talk was of how he'd set out in the spring
once the ice had cleared and his terror of snow
receded into its cave, how he'd spear
the winter months and cure them, save
the best of the apples, prepare good lengths
of rope to keep him safe whatever happened
then sit and speak with us about his deep
love of the sea.
                                        And indeed light had just
begun to fill the room and a faint white quality
of air to rise like a thin glass dome
over the town (though to us the ice
seemed solid still as stone) the day he came down
and taking with him nothing set out alone.

Quebec

Last night you called across the ice-pillow,
the question you'd been carving all winter.
Snow knife, air knife, the children deep in sleep.

Too chill for instruments, you sang: throat wreath
for a stilled land – rivers frozen like words
on the tongue, the vast bay, the terrifying cold.

So in this séance-season we each mourn,
nights back to back with night, or else turn,
the body closest on this silent plain

and lip to lip breathe winter's only answer –
the solitary owl in the darkness,
the beauty of the ice-journey, its flame.

No 3 from *Uses for the Thames*

"Feather!" cried the Sheep ...
– Lewis Carroll, 'Through the Looking-Glass'

The test was to dip
the needles into the dark
of the swallowing mirror

and by pulling to row
the weight of your own small self
through the silvery jam of its surface

trailing behind in your passing
your very own tale, knitted
extempore from light

and then to lift them,
feathered, ready for flight.

Surgeon

He swims just before dawn, breasting the river
like a hill, parting it with his arms like a dancer
or priest. Ahead, a flat line of light divides
the two dark halves of the world from each other.

The air leans up to his face and with his ears only
he senses the dark landscape of the water,
its prostrate fields and struggling hedges,
its low-lying ridges and flooded verges.

Below the surface pearls of half-light, silver
with oxygen, cling like prayer beads to his fingers.
He is thinking about the anatomy of the heart,
the forks in the road, the red caves and narrow lanes

and on the horizon the possibility of a cathedral,
the sun rising like a corpuscle, winter wheat.

from *Pearl*

Like the moment when the moon appears
before the dropping light of day
has cleared the evening sky, so I
became aware of a procession
in the city: wonderful and sudden,
with no sign or signal, the shining streets
were lined with virgins all adorned
in the very clothes my girl had worn.
The crowns they wore were like her crown,
their pearls and pure white dresses all
like hers, and at each maiden's breast
the same pure pearl of happiness.

Down every street and alleyway
of gold alight like glinting glass
they passed together in a stream
of happiness, one hundred thousand
dressed alike, not one less radiant
than the rest. And at their head the Lamb,
whose seven horns were flames
of reddened gold, whose garments shone
like precious polished pearls.
Thousands flowed towards the throne
in happiness – demure, meek
as young girls might behave at Mass.

I have no ready words to tell
what happiness his coming stirred:
as he approached, the elders fell
upon their knees before his feet
and angels in their legions threw
sweet smelling incense on the air.
Their voices were one single voice,
their vows one single vow of praise

toward the man they named their pearl.
That sound could strike from heaven down
through the very earth to hell. That sound
contained my happiness as well.

For now my mind was overwhelmed
with wonder at the sight of him –
how gentle and serene he seemed,
beyond the realms of any kind
of man I'd ever known before.
His robes were untouched white, his face
and features unassuming, full
of grace, and near his heart a wound
shone fresh, torn fiercely in his side,
his bright blood pouring from his pale flesh.
Who could delight in such a deed,
and not be seared by sorrow at the sight?

And yet his happiness was plain to all:
though wounded with his body torn,
the features of his face betrayed
no trace of pain but shone with bliss.
His brilliant retinue seemed charged
with life – and there she stood, my queen
who I thought still near me by the stream.
My God, she seemed so happy there
among her friends – the sight of her
so pale, so very white, drove me
toward the river, drawn on by desire
for her, by longing and by love.

– from Middle English,
14th-c. Anon.

DAVID FERRY

David Ferry's most recent collection is *Of No Country I Know* (University of Chicago Press). He has been awarded, among other prizes, the Lenore Marshall Prize from the Academy of American Poets and the Rebekah Johnson Bobbitt National Prize for Poetry from the Library of Congress. His translations include *Gilgamesh: A New Rendering in English Verse,* the *Odes of Horace,* the *Epistles of Horace*, the *Eclogues of Virgil*, and most recently the *Georgics of Virgil* (all Farrar, Straus and Giroux). He is completing a new book of poems and is translating Virgil's *Aeneid*. His wife was the eminent literary scholar Anne Ferry. "The Guest Ellen at the Supper for Street People," "The Proselyte," "Down by the River," and "Courtesy" are reprinted from *Of No Country I Know: New and Selected Poems and Translations,* copyright © 1999 by The University of Chicago, all rights reserved. (Photo courtesy of Stephen Ferry.)

The Guest Ellen at the Supper for Street People

The unclean spirits cry out in the body
Or mind of the guest Ellen in a loud voice,
Torment me not, and in the fury of her unclean
Hands beating the air in some kind of unending torment –
Nobody witnessing could possibly know the event
That cast upon her the spell of this enchantment.

Almost all the guests are under some kind of enchantment:
Of being poor day after day in the same body;
Of being witness still to some obscene event;
Of listening all the time to somebody's voice
Whispering in the ear things divine or unclean,
In the quotidian of unending torment.

One has to keep thinking there was some source of torment,
Something that happened someplace else, unclean.
One has to keep talking in a reasonable voice
About things done, say, by a father's body
To or upon the body of Ellen, in enchantment
Helpless, still by the unforgotten event

Enchanted, still in the old forgotten event
A prisoner of love, filthy Ellen in her torment,
Guest Ellen in the dining hall in her body,
Hands beating the air in her enchantment,
Sitting alone, gabbling in her garbled voice
The narrative of the spirits of the unclean.

She is wholly the possessed one of the unclean.
Maybe the spirits came from the river. The enchantment
Entered her, maybe, in the Northeast Kingdom. The torment,
A thing of the waters, gratuitous event,
Came up out of the waters and entered her body
And lived in her in torment and cried out in her voice.
It speaks itself over and over again in her voice,

Cursing maybe or not a familiar obscene event
Or only the pure event of original enchantment
From the birth of the river waters, the pure unclean
Rising from the source of things, in a figure of torment
Seeking out Ellen, finding its home in her poor body.

Her body witness is, so also is her voice,
Of torment coming from unknown event;
Unclean is the nature and name of the enchantment.

The Proselyte

A man the unclean spirits had gotten into
Got into the parish hall on Tuesday night.

The unclean spirits poured out through his skin
In the form of filth and cried out in that form,

And cried out in the form of how he went
Rapidly back and forth as if on many

Errands to one person and another
Or to nobody, up and down the parish hall,

Little trips back and forward rapidly,
Like a wasp or fly, hysterical with purpose,

Battering himself against our difference.
There was authority in him as he went

Carrying his message to one of us and another.
Who had condemned him to this filth and to

This unavailing rage? And the little voice
Crying out something in the body's cage?

The voice was pitifully small, as if
From someplace else or time of childhood, say,

Or country other, telling us something no one
In the parish hall could possibly understand,

Rabbinical, as if of ancient learning
Knowledgeable, and unintelligible,

A proselyte, the morphemes were uncouth.
His body was clad in the black of the unclean spirits.

And then he was gone away from the dining room,
A wasp trapped in a house, desperately trying,

Flying from one room into another room,
How to get out of the place in which it was,

Or else to carry the message to some place other.
He went to the phone on the wall of the hall outside

And said into the phone whatever it was he was saying;
And tore the phone out of the wall and talked to the wall,

Telling it things in the tiny faroff doleful
Insect crying voice in that other language.

And then he went to the outside door and said
To the outside door of the parish hall whatever

It was he said to us and the phone and the wall.
And then he was gone away into the night.

Down by the River

The page is green. Like water words are drifting
Across the notebook page on a day in June
Of irresistible good weather. Everything's easy.
On this side of the river, on a bench near the water,

A young man is peaceably stroking the arm of a girl.
He is dreaming of eating a peach. Somebody's rowing.
Somebody's running over the bridge that goes over
The highway beyond the river. The river is blue,

The river is moving along, taking it easy.
A breeze has come up, and somewhere a dog is barking,
Challenging the stirring of the breeze.
Nobody knows whose dog. The river is moving,

The boats are moving with it, or else against it.
People beside the river are watching the boats.
Along the pathway on this side of the river
Somebody's running, looking good in the sunshine,

Everything going along with everything else,
Moving along in participial rhythm,
Flowing, enjoying, taking its own sweet time.
On the other side of the river somebody else,

A man or a woman, is painting the scene I'm part of.
A brilliantly clear diminutive figure works
At a tiny easel, and as a result my soul
Lives on forever in somebody's heavenly picture.

Resemblance

It was my father in that restaurant
On Central Avenue in Orange, New Jersey,
Where I stopped for lunch and a drink, after coming away
From visiting, after many years had passed,
The place to which I'd brought my father's ashes
And the ashes of my mother, and where my father's
Grandparents, parents, brothers, had been buried,
And others of the family, all together.

The atmosphere was smoky, and there was a vague
Struggling transaction going on between
The bright day light of the busy street outside,
And the somewhat dirty light of the unwashed
Ceiling globes of the restaurant I was in.
He was having lunch. I couldn't see what he was having
But he seemed to be eating, maybe without
Noticing whatever it was he may have been eating;
He seemed to be listening to a conversation
With two or three others – Shades of the Dead come back
From where they went to when they went away?
Or maybe those others weren't speaking at all? Maybe
It was a dumbshow? Put on for my benefit?

It was the eerie persistence of his not
Seeming to recognize that I was there,
Watching him from my table across the room;
It was also the sense of his being included
In the conversation around him, and yet not,
Though this in life had been familiar to me,
No great change from what had been there before,
Even in my sense that I, across the room,
Was excluded, which went along with my sense of him
When he was alive, that often he didn't feel
Included in the scenes and talk around him,
And his isolation itself excluded others.

Where were we, in that restaurant that day?
Had I gone down into the world of the dead?
Were those other people really Shades of the Dead?
We expect that, if they came back, they would come back
To impart some knowledge of what it was they had learned.
Or if this was, indeed, Down There, then they,
Down there, would reveal, to us who visit them,
In a purified language some truth that in our condition
Of being alive we are unable to know.

Their tongues are ashes when they'd speak to us.

Unable to know is a condition I've lived in
All my life, a poverty of imagination
About the life of another human being.
This is, I think, the case with everyone.
Is it because there is a silence that we
Are all of us *forbidden* to cross, not only
The silence that divides the dead from the living,
But, antecedent to that, is it the silence
There is between the living and the living,
Unable to reach across that silence through
The baffling light there always is between us?
Among the living the body can do so sometimes,
But the mind, constricted, inhibited by its ancestral
Knowledge of final separation, holds back,
Unable to complete what it wanted to say.

What is your name that I can call you by?

Virgil said, when Eurydice died again,
"There was still so much to say" that had not been said
Even before her first death, from which he had vainly
Attempted, with his singing, to rescue her.

Courtesy

It is an afternoon towards the end of August:
Autumnal weather, cool following on,
And riding in, after the heat of summer,
Into the empty afternoon shade and light,

The shade full of light without any thickness at all;
You can see right through and right down into the depth
Of the light and shade of the afternoon; there isn't
Any weight of the summer pressing down.

In the backyard of the house next door there's a kid,
Maybe eleven or twelve, and a young man,
Visitors at the house whom I don't know,
The house in which the sound of some kind of party,

Perhaps even a wedding, is going on.
Somehow you can tell from the tone of their voices
That they don't know each other very well –
Two guests at the party, one of them, maybe,

A friend of the bride or groom, the other the son
Or the younger brother, maybe, of somebody there.
A couple of blocks away the wash of traffic
Dimly sounds, as if we were near the ocean.

They're shooting baskets, amiably and mildly.
The noise of the basketball, though startlingly louder
Than the voices of the two of them as they play,
Is peaceable as can be, something like meter.

The earnest voice of the kid, girlish and manly;
And the voice of the young man, carefully playing the game
Of having a grown up conversation with him.
I can tell the young man is teaching the boy by example,

The easy way he dribbles the ball and passes it
Back with a single gesture of wrist to make it
Easy for the kid to be in synch;
Giving and taking, perfectly understood.

Translation of Virgil, *Aeneid*, VI, ll. 305-329

A vast crowd, so many, rushed to the riverbank:
Women and men, famous great-hearted heroes,
The life in their hero bodies now defunct,
Unmarried boys and girls, sons whom their fathers
Had had to watch being placed on the funeral pyre;
As many as the leaves of the forest that,
When autumn's first chill comes, fall from the branches;
As many as the birds that flock in to the land
From the great deep when, the season, turning cold,
Has driven them over the seas to seek the sun.
They stood beseeching on the river bank,
Yearning to be the first to be carried across,
Stretching their hands out towards the farther shore.
But the stern ferryman, taking only this one,
Or this other one, pushes the rest away.

Aeneas cries out, wondering at the tumult,
"O virgin, why are they crowding at the river?
What is it that the spirits want? What is it
That decides why some of them are pushed away
And others sweep across the livid waters?"
The aged priestess thus replied: "Anchise's son,
True scion of the gods, these are the pools
Of the river Cocytos and this the Stygian marsh,
Whose power it is to make the gods afraid
Not to keep their word. All in this crowd are helpless
Because their bodies have not been covered over.
The boatman that you see is Charon. Those
Who are being carried across with him are they
Who have been buried. It is forbidden
To take any with him across the echoing waters
That flow between these terrible riverbanks
Who have not found a resting-place for their bones.
Restlessly to and fro along these shores

They wander waiting for a hundred years.
Not until after that, the longed-for crossing."

That Now Are Wild and Do Not Remember

Where did you go to, when you went away?
It is as if you step by step were going
Someplace elsewhere into some other range
Of speaking that I had no gift for speaking,
Knowing nothing of the language of that place
To which you went with naked foot at night
Into the wilderness there elsewhere in the bed,
Elsewhere somewhere in the house beyond my seeking.
I have been so dislanguaged by what happened
I cannot speak the words that somewhere you
Maybe were speaking to others where you went.
Maybe they talk together where they are,
Restlessly wandering along the shore,
Waiting for a way to cross the river.

JOHN FULLER

John Fuller's *Collected Poems* was published in 1996, and his *Stones and Fires* won the Forward Prize in 1997. The latest two of the six volumes of poetry written since then will appear in spring 2010: *Writing the Picture* (with photographs by David Hurn) from Seren Books, and *Pebble & I* from Chatto and Windus. His new pamphlet, *The Shell Hymn Book,* is now available from the Shoestring Press. He was Fellow and Tutor in English at Magdalen College, Oxford, from 1966 to 2002.

The Mechanical Body

Lifting a curl of its hair mounted on gauze,
Inserting the key into one ear oiled with its own wax,

You were at first surprised by its yielding and weight,
The way you could wind it to a pitch of response.

The whole mass trembled with released springs,
A shuddering at the heart of it like laughter.

It stunned the player with its fringed opening eyes,
Making the onlookers instinctively draw back.

But it was all surface and expedient dollwork,
With hidey-holes for soul and coils for motive.

The lacunae (. . .) (. . .) behind the knees,
The temporary leather, the hinged armpits,

Stencilled flowers on the linen ribs,
Your hands disappearing into glue.

Its sentiments worked on pulleys and punched rolls,
Tinny between bellows and horn-membrane.

The first hummings and trillings eased into
A pert sotto chirrup: 'Now then, Bertie!'

Little fans spun above the turning cylinders
And, with a tilt of the whirring chin and a slight click,

'Do it again, do it again, do it again' modulated
Into deeper, more thrilling pronouncements,

And whatever you cared to say came flatteringly back
From a library of teeth shining and uplifted

As the vibrations of the throat sang out their triumph
Of elocution: 'Tonight – cherry tart!'

That face was all-important, the ivory jaw
Traced in one chisel-sweep from lobe to lobe,

The nose a guardian of resonance, vellum temples,
The powdered cheeks borrowed from mandarin hangings,

Best was the mouth, embroidered minutely,
Hidden the hooks and wires that trembled it into motion.

Their working went deep into the busy centre
Of emptiness, as from the flies of a theatre:

Oiled strands trundled from a central gear
Slung between the rolling pivots of the hips.

The sounding vibrato of the belly concealed
The whine of its continual working.

Its long strings leading to that simple ring
Through which they fanned, the ring contracted

And its webs and skeins diversified into
A pursed amusement or a moue of disgust

Or turned inside-out like a cat's cradle,
Offering its watered-silk tapestry for kisses.

How the onlookers cheered! The thing was rooted,
Statuesque, a third larger than life.

It was gaunt with dust and tulle.
Bits of it glittered, even in the dark.

Great springs slowly lifted the padded knees,
Whiskery skirts leaking oil on to the floorboards.

And all the time was this ripple of felt and enamel,
This little jabbering of hammers and pulleys:

Its talking might talk you through till morning.
Your back was bruised from its attentions.

You thought of figureheads and oceans.
You thought of young mothers in their milk.

You thought of the egg-smooth backs of eyeballs
Staring unknowingly into the smoky caves of the future.

You thought of your life as a cheerful wager,
As a torn ticket of entry, a key to be used once.

You thought of cog turning cog turning cog,
The perpetual motion of the Last Chance.

You thought of the questioning of beauty in eternity,
Your hands at the controls, and celestial signs.

But as it wound down, its fingers barely twitching,
A tell-tale ticking from the ratchets of its joints,

There was nothing in the business but a blush,
A scattering of applause, a stillness.

And in that stillness, the postscript of a last
Creaking inch of clockwork was like a hollow laugh:

Hollow as the likeness of truth to a skull.
Hollow as the starlight pull of the doll.

Hope and Hearts

In the brown garden
Where playing lost its shadow
Among the lonely trees

These pale children of November
Rise from leaves
To forbid the frost and burning.

Frilfralog round the oaks
Tipsy and teetering
Putting up parasols

Skirted and stiff as dolls,
Never so still a dance,
So haunted a step

Till limp they lie down
Spilling their frills
In a lavish sprawl.

Everything goes back to earth
But first it must dance,
Dance to exhaustion.

They are our strangest thoughts,
Music of a mood
That will always create them

A solemn raggedy dance
At the year's end
But still as our own games

Games of outlandish endeavour
Games of promising
Games of hope and hearts

And like their rules
Allowing all they allow
And sometimes unbroken.

'Prudence dans L'Eau'

Far from being a warning,
Today's newspaper horoscope
Is simply a tender description
Of this aquarelle you enact
As if by a maître of 1919

For whom the maillot, beyond
Its masquerading as a garment,
Becomes the tracing of a line
Negotiating a containment
Of convalescent blue.

You may picture the sea
As a requirement of masses:
Here, the caution of shoulders
A shade of biscuit against
A disintegrating wall of wave.

There, the wide wash of azure
With its pucker of cobalt
And unsettling flung creams.
And further, just off-centre,
The teacherly red tick of a sail.

It's not that you're happy to become this picture.
You're happy for once to be yourself,
Cradled in water that moves for ever
Over the stones and fishes of the morning,
Beneath the stones and fires of night.

A Cuclshoc

Not the new racquets themselves, strung
To the pitch of drums in that wiry meshed black
Of loudspeakers. Not the crammed tube of feathers.

They are a daughterly indulgence, gear
To stir the sluggish pumps and muscles of our fifties,
Mythical as the breath they need, and tan knees.

Not these, which seem a flattering novelty,
But a letter found later in a dusty trunk
Brings to mind all that I know of this game.

Brings it back across a half century
In a cautious upper case and licked pencil
That once imagined Blackpool for Nairobi.

The signifiers are elementary. I HAVE
GOT A CUCLSHOC. I CAN HIT IT
5 TIMS. What else do I remember?

The cistern drip and chill of an attic Christmas.
The layered curves of the frames, stained maroon
Like spills, and trussed with yellow woven gut.

And the rattling thwung of the wobbly cork tub
Bound with its brittle stumps of varnished feathers
That however hard you hit it, slowed, and turned.

It made me think of the parson's nose, all quills:
When it wavered towards me over the washing-line
It was like getting ready to biff a chicken's bum.

And if I missed, although it had stopped dead
Mysteriously in mid-air, it dropped just too quickly
Out of my reach, like a newsreel commando.

Whatever I might have known about adult love,
About the sacred triviality of letters
Or their conspiracy at a distance about presents,

Whatever I suspected might be uncertain in the future,
In the size of oceans, the licensed irregularity
Of wars and the accuracy of torpedoes,

Cries out from these laborious sentences
With all their childish feeling and now with all
My later tears. I HOPE YOU WILL COM BACK SOON

SO WE CAN HAVE SOM FUN. That winged basket,
That little lofted button, forever hovering,
Still hangs in the back yard, beyond my racquet.

The feathers are splayed in the sun, like the fragile words
We sometimes write and mean, which therefore always
Mean and always will be there to do so.

SEND A FOTOGRAF OF YOR SELF. It glints
With the stitching of angels, buoyant in the light,
Never falling. WELL WELL GOOD BY DADDY DEAR.

Too Late

Summer of all seasons in its core
We feel to be wasted. It has passed
Almost unnoticed, like happiness.

How early it began! Earlier
Than we had realized, not too late
It seems, to take it fully to heart.

The welcome of a wood suffused
With bluebells which we never saw,
The mating of thrushes, thickening grass.

These things occurred while we were waiting
For them to occur, and leaves made shade
That still required the sun to prove it.

The year's tennis star is crouched
At the service line of his career.
The ball is dripping from his hand.

The gum of the sycamore is suspended
Like aerial gossamer above
My pile of examination scripts.

We are booked like actors to appear
At the triumphant opening:
The leaves are a superfluity of tickets.

We approach summer like conquerors
Entering a city already ravaged,
Hollow stems and dried blossoms.

Scorched grasses with lines of ants
Like native bearers, spikes and thorns,
The reek of pods and seeded herbs.

The exhalation of the summer,
Its reach and perfect stillness, the sea's
Calm at the close of a sandy path

Bearing a dab of white sail
Like a sudden excitement, all now
Forgotten, shut from the restless mind.

Now there will be no more of it.
Now pears bomb a vacant flower-bed
And garden wood is damp to the grasp.

Now we are in a mood to expect nothing
But the rich disappointment of the mood itself,
The heavy bending of a plant that is shed

Of its compulsions towards the receiving soil
And whose root now takes a grip of that dank chill
Even as its stalk springs lightly back.

Seven Vials

She gave me seven vials
Ranked in their colours, bright
As old flags once were.

The first had a dull glow,
Pale as the earliest flowers:
It weighed like a stone in my hand.

The second, a living green,
Seemed to have nowhere to go
But stirred like a leaf in my hand.

The third held a commonplace
Azure of emptiness
And died like hope in my hand.

The fourth was a ripe fruit
Trapped in its purple glass:
It stayed like a bruise on my hand.

The fifth with its stink of death
Laboured to shed its rust
And clung like ice to my hand.

The sixth contained embers
Of a vital distillation
And pulsed like a vein in my hand.

The seventh was the indigo
Of pure questioning
And moved like a hand in my hand.

These were to be poured
In order, and in order
To be for a time preserved.

Spilling and sometimes mixing,
Elements of the eternal
In the ceremony of life.

MARK HALLIDAY

Mark Halliday teaches at Ohio University. His books of poems are *Little Star* (1987), *Tasker Street* (1992), *Selfwolf* (1999), *Jab* (2002), and *Keep This Forever* (2008). His critical study of Wallace Stevens, *Stevens and the Interpersonal*, was published in 1991 by Princeton University Press. He has published essays on many poets, including Stevie Smith, Kenneth Koch, Michael Laskey, David Kirby, Kenneth Fearing, Claire Bateman, and Mary Ruefle, and he co-authors comic playlets with the British poet Martin Stannard. A chapbook of his poems entitled *No Panic Here* was published in 2009 by HappenStance Press in Fife, Scotland. (Photo courtesy of Jill Rosser.)

Summer Planning

My father and I on the sofa talked about summer plans,
would he drive from New York to Ohio?
It seemed doubtful (he was eighty-six)
and he said We'll see what comes to pass.
For a minute we were silent.
He said, That's an interesting idiom, isn't it.
To come to pass. "It came to pass."
There's a feeling of both coming and going at the same time.
Yeah, I said. I wondered what movie we might see.
He said, It's quite different to say "It happened" –
that sounds like a stop, like a fixed point.
But "It came to pass" – there's almost a feeling of
"It came in order to pass."
Yeah, I said, that's right.
He said, You get a sense of the transience of everything.
Yes, I said.
Cleo the black cat lay snoozing across my father's legs.
My father stroked her gently.
I finished my raspberry iced tea.

Chicken Salad

Everybody's father dies.
When it happens to someone else, I send a note of sympathy
or at least an e-mail. It's certainly worth the bother.
But when my father died, it was *my father.*

*

Three hours before he died
my father felt he should have an answer
when I asked what he might like to eat.
He remembered a kind of chicken salad he liked
weeks ago when living was more possible
and he said "Maybe that chicken salad"
but because of the blood in his mouth
and because of his shortness of breath
he had to say it several times before I understood.
So I went out and bought a container of chicken salad,
grateful for the illusion of helping,
but when I brought it back to the apartment
my father studied it for thirty seconds
and set it aside on the bed. I wasn't ready
to know what the eyes of the nurse at the Hospice
had tried to tell me before dawn, so I said
"Don't you want your chicken salad, Daddy?"
He glanced at it from a distance of many miles –
little tub of chicken salad down on the planet of
slaughtered birds and mastication, digestion, excretion –
and murmured "Maybe later." He was in
the final austerity
which I was too frazzled to quite recognize
but ever since his death I see with stony clarity
the solitary dignity of
the totality of his knowing
how far beyond the pleasure of chicken salad
he had gone already and would go.

*

Everybody's father dies; but
when my father died, it was my father.

Walking the Ashes

When I picked up my father's ashes
at Crestwood Memorial Chapel downtown
the box was astoundingly heavy
just as everyone always says about human ashes
and besides he was a big man – but still

I wanted to walk with him for a while –
to see how it felt to walk with his ashes
through streets he walked so vigorously in the Thirties,
the noisy exciting Thirties which were the present then

so we set out in the sunshine.
A restaurant near the corner of Spring and Mott
had Specials on a sidewalk chalkboard
and the top Special was Salmon Affumicato with Vodka Cream
and I said "That sounds good"
but the ashes said "Maybe a little too fancy."

My father liked his pleasures bold and clear and decisive;
he used to say the way to throw a good party was to roast
a big ham and put it on the table with a sharp knife
and let everybody just hack off chunks

and he made me feel sort of effete at times;
but he also inspired me to love my own opinions.
The sun blazed and my arms began to hurt
but we kept walking for at least thirty blocks, comparing notes;

I kept suggesting that the day was bright with meaning
but the ashes suspected it was all absurdly blank,
all drained of something grand that Benny Goodman once expressed.
We agreed in admiration of certain women on their lunch hour,
but the ashes muttered something about beauty being
an intolerable trick in a world that turns you eighty-nine years old.

"Well, Daddy, I'm still on my feet" I said
but it was hot and my arms did hurt so I hailed a cab.

The ashes on the back seat of the cab were quiet
and I was quiet, we let New York stream past the windows,
let it go, because even the most vigorous walkers
with the most emphatic opinions
will eventually need a break from the world.

The Sunny Ridge

In my dream my mother was alive, talking with her friend
Madame de Piolenc, in beach chairs on a sandy ridge
just outside a screened enclosure of shade. They sat
in mild sunshine talking intently; and I knew they were
there, though I was with others down the hill
in some clacking room of noise like a small train station
and the people all wanted to relocate, for further fun,
they were flapping like ducks with sunglasses,
they were caught up in the pleasing social confusion
and they said "Come on here we go" but I said
"I have to get my mother"
                                        so she would not miss
the picnic or whatever and they all understood
so then I walked fast among pines up the shady hill
carrying a shishkabob skewer loaded with tomatoes and onions
and I entered the screened enclosure and blinked,
then through the shady screen I saw my mother,
saw her brown hair so lightly streaked with strands of white
over the back of her beach chair where she leaned
a little sideways to listen to Madame de Piolenc,
so then I moved carefully through the door trying
not to disturb other people who sat on the sunny ridge,
anxious not to poke them with my loaded skewer;
and my blue shirt snagged on a hook but only
for a second and then
                                    I did reach my mother,
she and Madame de Piolenc smiled because I seemed anxious
and because their conversation had been so wry and amusing
and I did tell my mother about the picnic
and how much everyone hoped she'd rejoin the group.

The Drift

In 1932 Lois and Milt danced laughing, Lois showing Milt the steps,
to a tune called "Street of Dreams"
and in 1993 a song called "Book of Dreams"
brought tears to my eyes because for a minute it meant everything
about the failure of my first marriage
and the aching faith that would have to make me ready
for my second marriage
and in 1968 Cathy and I gleamed at each other
through the light sweet fragile notes of "Dream a Little Dream of Me"
and in 1904 there was a song "Picnic in Dreamland"
that Connie sang with Herb while waiting for a Baltimore train
that carried him, as it turned out, to new involvements
and there was no way to know in 1959 what it could mean
for me and Marcia who lived across the street
when Bobby Darin sang "Dream lover, where are you?"
okay, okay we see, we catch the drift,
you don't have to give us any more examples

mist swells thick over the sleeping field
till it's gone above the steady rooted trees.

Lois in the Sunny Tree

When in August 1920 I smiled for the camera
from my perch on the limb of a sun-spangled tree,
says Lois, long dead now but humorously seven years old then,
with a giant ribbon in my hair, the sorrow of living in time
was only very tiny and remote in some far corner of my mind

and for me to know then, as I smiled for that camera
in Michigan in the summer of 1920
that you would peer thoughtfully and admiringly
into my happy photographed eyes eighty-some years later
would have been good for me only in a very tiny and remote way.

Down Here

We tried being together; after a while it felt like a mistake.

We sat with tea in her kitchen. She said,
"I know that poetry can be very interesting
and I know it makes some people happy and that's fine
but what I can't relate to, in the end,
is the whole idea of plucking something *out* of *life,*
the idea of removing some little piece of life
from the whole messy flow of everything –
the way you think you need to sort of isolate this one bit of
        experience
in this sort of glass box that you call a poem –
you want to put it in the box
and hoist the box to a top shelf way up
where grubby time won't smudge it –
time with its grubby money and plastic bags of garbage
and people who say they care about you and then don't
and skin fungus and gum disease and arthritis
and car engines breaking down and hospital rooms
and people getting addicted to things –
you think you can put even anybody's mother with Alzheimer's
or anybody's uncle with diabetes or any other piece of the world
into the crystal box if you just trim it to fit – "

(I could see from her face that she liked her metaphor
of the crystal box on the high shelf
and she hoped it was a good enough metaphor
so that I would remember it and remember her for it)

" – and what I can't relate to is the whole assumption
that you can do that and then things are somehow all better
when actually they're not because actually there *is* no top shelf,
I mean everything is *down here* and everything dies.
The poems that you're always poking at are pieces of paper
that end up in boxes – *cardboard* boxes –

and the boxes eventually get hauled to a dumpster
by the teenage boys working for your granddaughter's landlord
or the teenage boys helping to clear out a warehouse or a library
basement
maybe thirty years from now, maybe sixty, and they end up as
landfill
just like you and me and all our friends, we're all on our way
to being landfill – and what we really need
is for us to be decent to each other and if possible
to be generous and kind. And those words are boring to you – "

(her voice was now trembling and she was striving not to cry
and I almost realized I was glad to be important enough
to make her nearly cry about this)

" – which is why what I'm saying is not a poem.
Which is why poems are not what I care about because
to me what counts is for people to notice how other people are
feeling
and to respond to that *right then* and for people to give each other
little surprise presents and to phone someone and say 'How are you
doing'
in a real way and to talk to people about what matters to them
outside your own little world of crystal treasures.
That's what I look for in a person and what happens is,
we do our best and ultimately a few people visit us in the hospital
and then we die."

She stopped and looked away and calmed her breathing.

I thought: I respect her; but I don't think I can love her.
Or, not romantically. And I thought how much worse I would feel
if she had said all of this without getting upset.

(She had a way of rapidly tapping her cheekbone with one finger
to keep back tears when she thought tears would be sentimental;
I remembered loving her for that; I saw
how someone else could love that soon.)

I looked down
I gazed down
Down I gazed
Down gazed I into my cold cup of tea.

Ask Wendy Wisdom

Dear Wendy Wisdom,

My second marriage ended a few years ago. My daughter grad-
    uated from college
this year. Lately I feel lost. I keep thinking there's someone I could
    meet
who would make my life exciting and important.
But when I have dinner with friends of friends,
the restaurant roars like a wind-tunnel of mutual boredom.
I keep using Google to locate people I dated, or had crushes on,
twenty or thirty years ago. But of course they turn out to have
    spouses, kids, lives,
they don't feel a craving to reconnect with me – only a brief
    curiosity.
Their e-mails say "How nice to hear from you" – but their messages
    get
shorter and shorter; the fourth message is nothing but
"Hope things work out!" In coffeeshops I see attractive individuals;
I think I sometimes stare at them too long. Once or twice
I've followed someone along a snowswept sidewalk
trying to think of something to say – "Would you like another
    decaf mocha?"
I feel invisible. I feel like a coat on a second-hand rack. I feel
like wet snow clinging to the side of a mail truck. What do you
    suggest?

– Mopey in Minneapolis

Dear Mopey,

First of all, moping is extremely unattractive.
The only reliable way to make oneself attractive is through
sustained intense interest in some subject (other than romance and
    sex).

Sustained intense interest is impossible to fake. Meanwhile,
you need to consider that relationship with another actual person
may not be able to give you the sense of visibility, significance, importance
you long for. Certainly if the idea of relationship is for you
essentially a conduit toward orgasm, your quest is doomed
by its objective. Orgasm is terribly overrated. It is chemically addictive,
but like other drugs it betrays you and leaves you grimacing in the bathroom.
If orgasm is what your daydreams basically hanker toward,
the only cure is old age – if that. Meanwhile,
it's true there are probably persons in the world with whom you could have
a fabulously meaningful and fulfilling friendship. Think of Emma Thompson
as she seems – the real-person equivalent of Emma Thompson probably does exist
within twenty miles of where you live in Minneapolis. But
you are very unlikely to find her. Therefore
what I suggest to you is: *representation*. Create
representations of your loneliness, your lostness, your boredom, your moping.
You seem to be good with words, so do your representing in words.
Represent the ice-crusted streets, the streetlights seen through wet windshields,
the vapid conversations about the Vikings and college tuition fees and sitcoms
and the brevity of years, also represent the alarming streaks of intelligence
that appear in some conversations, also the ponytailed waitress
whose smile transcends her expert curtness and whom you overhear
telling a waiter "I'm still living with Ashley and Gina – not alone –
'cause when I'm alone I just cry all the time." Represent
all this in great detail. Also represent the experiences, encounters you wish
could happen. Represent them with fierce attention to detail.
Elaborate your representations so richly that a reader can virtually

live in them!
Then let that reader be your dear companion.
Imagine that reader sitting thoughtfully beside a lamp on the far
side of the room.

– Wisely yours,
Wendy Wisdom

SASKIA HAMILTON

Saskia Hamilton is the author of two collections of poetry, *As for Dream* (2001) and *Divide These* (2005), and is at present working on *Night-Jar,* a sequence from which several of these poems come. She is the editor of *The Letters of Robert Lowell* (2005) and co-editor of *Words in Air: The Complete Correspondence of Elizabeth Bishop and Robert Lowell* (2008). She has received fellowships from the National Endowment for the Arts and the Guggenheim Foundation, and is associate professor of English at Barnard College, Columbia University. She lives in New York. (Photo courtesy of Julia Hamilton.)

Elegy

The work of burial is never done. First the interruption,
then the interruption, so it's carried on in sleep,
over to argument, floating in the water with the flowers
the shit the shells the debris from the city after the rains
have washed it to the beaches and the sea
has taken it up into itself. The figure with the shovel:
the figure with the shovel: the figure with
the book, the shoulders rising, the dog reading news
on the pavement washed then by rain running off the asphalt
down into the gulley where it goes under the city with the tunnelling

animals, the cunning animals, the readers under
the city.

Entrance

No one in the house but the two, the one
on the way to death, the other
on the way to earth. Above, the white sky
not ready to rain, below, lush,
the mid-summer garden, the thrush, or
the young of the thrush, or the seventeenth-
generation listed smaller thrush.

Below, a door opens. No one moves about
but you, in the white chair, typing.

Listen

The shaded window.
Voices from the garden rose to
the room and soon the green blanket
soothed you. The phone rang. A door
closed. No one turning
down the gravel path, no one
taking up the garden shears.

The Chair

If the chair were to be moved again,
it would find its own weight damaging.
It stands beside the chest. Its cloth
is worn away. Its brass fingers
keep a grip on things. Who would sit in it?
Who would read for a while beside it?

Entrance

Then I went indoors.
First came the beautiful one, whose
only thought was to stop. Then came
the beautiful one, who lay in the grass.
There followed the five beautiful ones
who brought shovels and spades. Lastly,
there was you. You looked from the window.
We said the one no to each other
that was required. The ones that followed
swept them up, the two negatives. Open, open.

from *Night-Jar*

[I]

Hawking for moths at dusk: the night-jar
in the fen near the worn stone markers
of the old bishopric: thence ceded
to sentries of the forest: thence the fall,
one by one: thence centuries under-
foot of branch and brush and peat. Near you,
but where, it has gone: past the rides.

[II]

January rain, thunder, odd season;
the day is over over there;

a dog bays at traffic; trucks
come up the road from the bridge,
bearing heads of lettuce to the city;

rain falters, lessens; 'then much,
then little, then nothing';

you are sleeping now, undone
in the bedclothes over there.

[III]

She made a cup of tea and took up
pencil and book, reading lines aloud,
ticking the good ones. She then
smoked half a cigarette, pinched it closed,
put it back in the packet.
It's probably a big mistake,
she said aloud, but couldn't place the remark.

*

My bad conscience was nothing other
than terrible vanity, he said in interview.
And I was terribly cruel. So
I don't have anything to do
with conscience now. They went
outdoors and stood by the boats
on shore pointing at outness.

*

When the phone rang, she spoke to her sister
for hours. I would go so far as
to say, she would say. She watched
as neighbors from across the way
moved past their windows.
The room grew darker. Insofar as,
she would say. She went as far as that.

[IV]

I dreamt I wrote to x around
the borders of a piece of hatched
paper he had written on; alternate
wheat and fallow, some

exhaustion land. It is said that,
after paradise, after a time,
the unfallen animals came down
the road and went

their separate ways: peacock, boar,
pheasant, rabbit; small birds roved
the fields and hedges; expanding under-
storeys of holly in woodlands;

spitting rain. Successes and lapses.
Plots halve in the drawing:
plans for second-floor passages
in the first house. Wheat begins growing.

After *'Gewritu secgað þæt seo wiht sy'*

It is written in scriptures that this
creature appears plainly to us
when the hour calls,
while its singular power compels
and confounds our knowing.
It seeks us out, one by one,
following its own way; fares on,
with its stranger's step, never
there a second night, native
to no place; moves according
to its nature. It has no hands,
no feet, has never touched the ground,
no mouth to speak of,
nor mind. Scriptures say
it is the least of anything made.
It has no soul, no life, but travels
widely among us in this world;
no blood nor bone, but
consoles all the children of men.
It hasn't reached heaven,
it won't touch hell,
but takes instruction from
the king of glory. The whole story
of its fate – limbless as it is,
animate – is too obscure to tell.
And yet all the words we find
to describe it are just and true.
If you can say it, call it
by its rightful name.

GEORGE KALOGERIS

George Kalogeris teaches English Literature and Classics in Translation at Suffolk University in Boston, Massachusetts. He is the author of a book of poems based on the life and notebooks of Albert Camus, *Camus: Carnets* (Pressed Wafer, 2006). His poems and translations have appeared in *Literary Imagination, Poetry,* the *Oxford Gazette, Agni, Modern Greek Poetry in Translation,* the *Warwick Review, Ploughshares, Seneca Review,* the *Harvard Review, Salamander,* and *Little Star.* Recently, he completed a manuscript of paired poems in translation with a preface by Rosanna Warren (*Dialogos*). He received a PhD in Comparative Literature from the University Professors Program at Boston University in 1991. (Photo courtesy of Katherine Jackson.)

Leopardi: Saturday Night in the Village

As soon as the sun has set, that young woman
Returning from the fields, the one who goes
To the festival every Sunday, has already picked
The handful of flowers she'll wear tomorrow,
And carries them home with a bundle of kindling. Now
That the day is over she has the violets
She needs to arrange her hair, and the roses to match
Her dress, the dress that she'll wear tomorrow.

Sitting on the steps of her house, the old woman
Facing the dusk picks up a thread
Of her neighbor's conversation and turns all their talk
About tomorrow to the way it was
In her day, and the dresses she wore, and all the men
That were mad about her; the old woman
Spinning her yarns about how light she was
On her feet, her face radiant at dusk.

Already the darkness is filling the air we breathe;
Already the sky is no longer azure;
Now the hills are shadowed by the slopes of evening;
Now the new moon is just beginning
To turn the rooftops white, as if the houses
Were marked with chalk; and now and again
The mouth of a clanging bell is telling us something
We already know: tomorrow is Sunday.

Still, when church bells ring the heart can't help
Feeling a lift as the little children
Swarm the little piazza, shouting on the run
As if they were heralds of leaping joy.
And even the farmer whistling to himself
As the bells chime with the end of his day
In the fields, couldn't look any happier, relishing what's left
Of those scraps he'll call supper when he gets home.

Sunday, the day of rest, cannot come fast
        Enough for the laborer, though it'll be over
Before he knows it. And now the lights of the houses
        Have all gone out, and the whole village
Is in the dark, not a murmur out of anyone –
        Except for the rasping sound of a saw
That works as they sleep, or the hammer blow that wakes
        The startled heart to its own pounding.

Which means the carpenter cannot yet afford
        To call it a day unless he has finished
One more job, polishing the grain of the wood
        Until it gleams without a trace
Of the sweat and blood it cost him; and dreading the light
        That shines through the cracks when Sunday dawns
On his shuttered windows, just as the dimming lantern
        Tells him it's time to close up shop.

Seven days of the week and only one
        That everyone always looks forward to
With a genuine sigh of relief. But when Sunday
        Finally arrives the mind is already
Drained by the usual concerns of the coming week,
        As if weariness and worry were the only
Outcomes we can always count on. Seven days,
        And this happiness that never stays

Longer than the little while it spends with us
        On Saturday evening…Little boy
So full of joy, so like this hour so like
        A flower whose blossom can bloom no further:
Do you know that the richest feast of your life is spread
        Before your eyes like clear blue skies
To an open bud? Enjoy it to the hilt,
        Because this is your moment of ultimate bliss.

About what happens next, I'd rather not say.
        But don't lose any sleep, my little friend,
Waiting for that festival they celebrate on Sunday.

Lucretius: Atomic Movement

And now I'd like to show you how such tiny
Particulars are moving. Once atoms take shape
As something, no matter what it is, Nature

Will never allow it to rise without the help
Of something else. Nothing can lift itself.
Don't let the hovering flame that seems composed

Of weightless particles fool you. All things are drawn
Inexorably to earth. And yet, we must also
Acknowledge that shining clusters of trees and crops

Have sprung from seeds, as if they were born to surge
Towards the sky. And just as a leaping flame
Can reach a roof-beam, and lick along the rafters

Until that voracious tongue devours the house,
So in the very same way a crimson spray
Of blood may gush from a wound, all but exultant

As it arches through the air. But don't assume
That either the fire or the blood can ever do this
Spontaneously: they always need some other

Force to reinforce them. Haven't you noticed
How powerfully a pool of water expels
Thick planks of wood? However many hands

Are shoving those planks down the water's throat, the water
Insists on vomiting them back up at us –
As if it delighted in seeing the wood buoyant

Enough to break the surface by half a length.
(Though the wood could never have done this without the water.)
And yet, beyond a shadow of doubt, atoms

Are always streaming away, just dense enough
To sink in a vacuum, down and away they go
En masse through empty space. And fire, it stands

To reason, is no exception. Fire is a clear
Expression of something that strives to rise in the air
That shimmers around us. Yet light as fire is,

The weight of its atoms is heavy enough to drag
It down incessantly. Don't you see how dark
The night would be without those blazing torches

Ascending the heavens? Yet even at the height
Of evening, their fiery wake only tracks the course
Laid out for them by Nature, from whose guidance

The torches of nightfall take their lead each night.
And when the night is over, isn't it obvious
That all that's left of all that impending gloom

Has dropped out of sight – along with all the stars
And the streaking meteors? As soon as the open fields
Have seen the light of day, the sun is already

Radiant enough to turn the farthest furrow
Golden by noon. And then the sun sinks back
To earth, as it must. Which only goes to show

That light, no matter how high it shines in the sky,
Is bound to descend, just like everything else.
Steeped in torrential rain, the lightning slants

Precipitously. But first it's the glow of cloudburst,
Spreading like wildfire across the darkening sky
As it crackles overhead. Then the abrupt bolt

Flashes like rods of the fasces in thunder's grip.
Lightning, as everyone should know by now,
Can strike at any place, and at any time.

Finally, there's one more point regarding matter
That I wish to convey: even as atoms are falling
Through empty space, each one dropping down

Straight as a plumb line, and carried along by the pull
Of its own weight, at certain moments they swerve
Together ever so slightly, and though it's just

Enough to say that a change in direction occurred,
We can never predict where and when it will happen.
And if this swerving never happened, then atoms

Would never collide with one another; and since
Creation depends on the unpredictable impact
Of colliding atoms, Nature would then have created

Nothing, though the atoms themselves would still
Be falling through empty space, falling like drops
Of rain falling by themselves forever.

Mandelstam: As I Was Washing Myself in the Dark (#126)

As I was washing myself in the dark,
Washing outside where the ice-cold water
Kept spilling over the rim of the barrel,

The evening stars against the horizon
Glistened like salt on the blade of an axe.
As I was washing myself in the dark,

I saw the locked gate that couldn't keep out
The menacing look of my surroundings,
Once it had entered my state of mind.

Soon the weavers will weave a new pattern
From anything they can get their hands on,
Looming there, in the near future:

No matter what fabric they happen to stitch
I don't think the seams will ever be finer
Than a single line of honest speech.

Salt of the earth and stars of the sky
Dissolving now in the water's reflection,
This briny water that keeps turning blacker,

Like some purer shade of appalling death –
As if our lips had already tasted
What's steeped in the salt of worsening luck.

As I was washing myself in the dark,
Washing outside where the ice-cold water
Kept spilling over the rim of the barrel,

The earth edged closer to truth and terror.

Selections from *Camus: Carnets*

5

Halfway between poverty and the sun
is how you described growing up in Algiers,
dirt-poor as the glistening dunes of the beach at Sablettes
where you learned to swim in a school of dolphins –
until dusk, when the *jeune filles* slithered away,
though your legs were still tangled in the seaweed's hair.

The Grecian urn before the age of images,
when the daughter of Dibutades, the potter, traced
the dusky line of a young man's shadow on a blank wall.
Silhouette for the first clay vase fired by Eros.
We lose track of the light, the body's hymnal.
The silent mouths of those who forgive themselves.

32

All winter long you waited for the eyes of the almonds
that open overnight, and there was nothing absurd
about waking to find the entire *Vallée des Consuls*
blanketed with white flowers, in late February.
And now the anonymous stand in their icy cells
and grip the bars. Their silence is never far away.

Amphitheater of the hills: the Eye of *Dike*
already clouded but the beams still palpably warm –
justice *in absentia* even as the stony palm
of evening is pressed to the troubled heart. The stranger
estranged from all but the *tender indifference of nature*.
Algeria's jagged cliffs. The sea more fraying at dusk.

66

The Facel-Vega picking up speed. Hairpin turns
twenty kilometers or so outside of Sens,
where the trees grow dense. Dappled pools by the curbing.
Horsepower in tune with the constellation of the lyre.
Then a ribbed nave of conifers. Or a shirt of fire.
Champigny-sur-Yonne like the blur of being young.

Suddenly in slow motion the shaggy chestnut reared
its crown of unshakeable affirmation. Gide
rustling toward you in slippers, stroking his tabby cat
Sarah. Those darkest years you shared his flat.
Then sudden impact. Focus on the sunlight like fur
growing fuzzy. Your shattered torso turning centaur.

Origins

Behind the words there is a poem
Behind the poem there is a voice
Behind the voice there is a breath
Behind the breath there must be silence
Behind the silence is where the voice
That speaks the poem is coming from

Inside the thirst there is a well
Inside the well there is no light
Inside the dark there is an echo
Inside the echo there must be longing
Inside the longing is where the water
No bucket can hold is coming from

MARCIA KARP

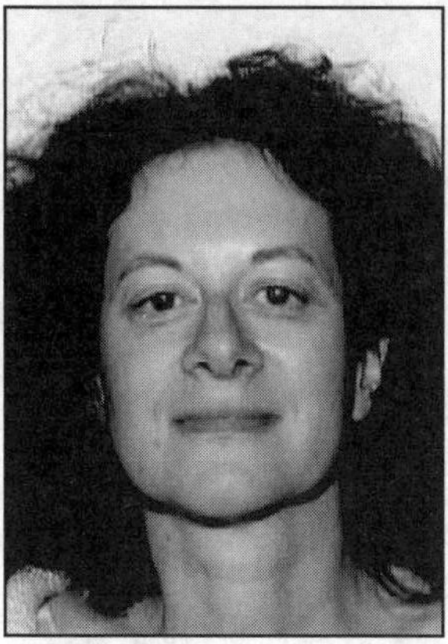

For Lois, who knows a thing or two or... about poems. With love, Marcia

Marcia Karp has poems and translations in *Partisan Review, The Republic of Letters, Literary Imagination, Catullus in English* (Penguin), *The Guardian, Seneca Review, Petrarch in English* (Penguin), *Agenda, Harvard Review, Ploughshares, The Warwick Review, The Word Exchange: Anglo-Saxon Poems in Translation* (Norton), and the *Times Literary Supplement*. Her doctoral work within the field of literary history – on the ordering of volumes of poems (*In Order: To Read a Poem*) – was undertaken at Boston University, where she now teaches. (Photo courtesy of Boston University.)

Evening Dance Class

for Debra

You forget you have told me this three weeks running, and
I can see you slower than the others,
afraid of putting the wrong foot forward
and back, to the side, tap the toe twice,
then the heel.

I see you stretching too long to the left,
palms down when they should be up,
the line of the newly enrolled moving here
and you still there.

I see the swell of your ankle and tears
and you, counting and keeping together
with the intruders as best you can,
ignored now, neither stopping nor dancing.

I can even see you writing your letter,
telling your teacher how hurt you are
to be now left behind.

But I can't, because you close the door and
play the music for yourself alone,
see you just later, in spin, in time, alone, in tune,
held up light and lithe by your wrists in graceful sweep, afraid,
in your dance, of no one and nothing.

Catastrophe

Here I have been out-Peneloping Penelope –
though not a husband, yet a brother,
and I've thirty-five years to her twenty,
no suitors, and about my life the loosed ends fray.
On the weekend, the last of us, me,
was reading in the sunshine from his schoolboy copy
as Odysseus makes himself known bit by bit.
From the right, not an eagle from Zeus,
but a lady-bug, traveling bug, far from her home,
rifles the pages ahead, flies from me, taking
the shape of the wind.
Penelope questions the stranger.
He is tricked into the tale of the bedpost.
She knows him. Hurrah.

And then grief (and I quote): Penelope speaks –
Think
what difficulty the gods gave: they denied us
life together in our prime and flowering years,
kept us from crossing into age together.

In his schoolboy pen he'd marked
(just the sixth mark in the book) these lines.
He'd bracketed the four together,
as well as the inside two (those twice).
I had to turn my face from Ithaka,
and marvel at this, a sign, the first
through all these years, that he'd know of our cowls of sorrow,
and knowing, would not have bid us wear them,
and so, he is dead, dead decades ago,
could not have let us suffer.

Had the gods not been rinsed from our world long ago
It might have been wayfinder Hermes in lady-bug sandals

Marking that passage while feast turned to massacre under my eyes.
But the boy marked the passage, and he is dead now I know:
Son of once-adamant mother, self-abjected father.
They never bewailed at his bier, nor I.

Or, you, O my brother, made hidden farewell
On the margins of our fortune. Content.
Your passage craftily marked, our lives clanging upon us.

Brother

Multas per gentes ... frater
– Catullus

Driven through people and people and places
  I am come to this terrible service   brother
so I might give you your last gift   the death gift
  might talk to your ashes   might listen in vain for their voice
Since your life took you from me   seized you
  unjust   brother   misery   took you from me
now   as we were taught by our parents   here
  I offer my last gift   a death gift
take it   wrapped only in brotherly tears
  and always   my brother   now I have found you   farewell

Ad Libitum

I like the dark and the air through the window
and the lamp on its arm – the one outside
and the one by my right hand, clamped to the desk.
I like the breeze and the heat it doesn't displace.
I like the typing and wish it were writing,
and I don't care as much as I should.
I like the every-so-often confusion of sounds:
the chair being rubbed by the desk, the cat,
a night bird at the feeder, my stomach.
I am pleased to roll to the reference book shelf
and pleased to pick, over there in the dark,
the right volume for "digestive." My guess
at the root was wrong: not *gusto* for taste,
but *gero* for carry. *Di-* for apart:
to tear, to divide. Authorities differ, but maybe
di-viduo, whence *widow*, *widower* –
to tear in the eye and the heart.
Still, words are not poems.
What I would like now is to stop.
The typing is fun, but it is, after all,
writing I want. Still, I am pleased by the sound
and the move of the keys, except when they lock,
and the carriage is nice on its creak of return.
The keys have three greens, but it is writing I am after.
I like its being my neighbors parking the car,
not strangers peering at lives behind windows,
some with screens on, but not all with them on.
I'll bet it looks romantic at this corner of a dark house,
a late night in June, the weather finally in season.
I am grateful this house,
bequeathed by a family to me, its youngest –
now, only – has chairs and books all over,
so when and in whichever I want,
I may sit and read or sit and write or sit and sit.

Tabula Rasa

I wrote the history of poetry
and prose. Of poesy and prosery
I wrote. Not all of it, just little bits
I chose, although I thought about what I'd
left out and wrote again and wrote some in.
I tried to write, in prose, what writers know
of craft. In prose go straight. But hesitate
in poems.
                Just like a child, my hands were drenched
in ink and paper balls of scrawling round
my feet were calling *Read me.* Some I'd read
again, and reading, knew that knowing prose
and poetry in history was far
from what I knew.
                        My tongue, my English tongue.
I closed my eyes and closed my hands so I
might hear how English spoke on all those tongues.
And underneath the tongues there is a mind
that has no words. It's there that language is.
And that – above my English tongue, the his-
tory of poetry and prose, the po-
ems, prose, the knowing – that arose to call me. O.

Mercy

Did you know, do you remember now, "the rat race"? –
honest, disinterested God in that lab coat
and stinky meats to send us, amazed, ascurry.
The first shall be first and the last shall go hungry
or hang, was the theme. Not a god for all time,
that clipboarded watcher, and too antiseptic for ours.

Mounted now each on the god who is God of the gods,
the tune is "On Vengeance. On Destiny. Gee-hup."
and a brutal whip hand on the flank of each courser.
At the races, no doubts; and the rich have the right
of way and the poor are left the dust. Never mind.

One of the old gods was born as a winnow wind
and each of us blew toward some runnel to outrace the flood
of our lives. It was good for the gods and remains
so: the first should be best, for the rest are as beasts.

It's Showtime

Come on – see the woman who keeps to herself.
There, right there, the standing-place woman

I saw her get kissed and she saw that I saw.
He wound up her hair. He commanded her jaw.
But she winked as I watched her allow him to brute her.
He didn't think if he might or not suit her.
There, (my dear), *she could withstand embrace*

One tried behavior to coax her to knowledge.
She held out for love. She refused to acknowledge
His presents of mind. "Only these!" would she ask,
Blearing and smearing her COME … NO, GO mask.
Wear, and tear, the demanding-face woman

The staging was stagnant – ONE WOMAN ALONE. STILL.
The one cue for some drama was scrawled on the play bill:
GET ANGRY. She rued it, but knew it was so:
The excitement of rage, or the self-keeping woe.
Soon here (do you hear?), she'll take it ill and give chase

Erratatum

I knew a drummer when I was a girl
and he was a man, who told me his rattattattat.
They'd never had anything like me, he said,
– ensnared not from love, but from art – among their beaten men.

Though we kissed after hotdogs and tasted of mustard,
his rolls and his flams and his tattattattoos
never sounded between us – the girl from one side,
the man from the other, of town.

He's still a man, if still he is.
I'm now a woman in grief for her art.
My tittle, my jot, have been scraped from my song.
They are mine and are perfect.
Stolen, my least sheep, my grace-notes, my ruffles.

I've always remembered that man from our vinegar kiss,
and his report – not the first, but the first I'd heard,
as he brushed by in kindness my life – of unmuffled madness from
art,
that, if I dare master the rattamacue, might be mine.

I Won't Mind It Then

I won't mind it, if at the last I overhear in the room
"Will you, do you think, get another Marcia when this one is ..."
because, no matter the quiet or the *not now, can't you see* that follows,
I would then be someone with someone who loves me enough
to want in the moment if appetite returns
that then, just then in mid-hum, I would die,
so we'd both – I'd be part of a both! – be sorry I was dead,
not wrung out of sorrow by the diapering,
slobbering, gibbering mess of the long overdue.

JENNY LEWIS

Jenny Lewis trained at the Ruskin School of Art before reading English at St Edmund Hall, Oxford. She has published two collections of poetry – *When I Became an Amazon* (Iron Press, 1996 and Bilingua Russia, 2002) and *Fathom* (Oxford*Poets*/Carcanet, 2007) – and has had seven plays and poetry cycles performed at theatres across Britain, extracts of which have been broadcast by the BBC. She teaches poetry at Oxford University and is an External Examiner for Creative Writing at York University. Her new verse drama, *After Gilgamesh,* will be performed at Pegasus Theatre, Oxford in 2011. (Photo courtesy of Ian Cole.)

Woman Brushing Her Hair

after Degas

In spring, I lived underwater with it –
my dappled hands held auburn hanks
like uncoiled ropes to brush and brush
while my thoughts drifted upwards
into the pearly green and umber.

By summer, my face was a scribble –
no eyes, a mute mouth, I forced the auburn
from its lair at the nape of my neck,
brushed it over my brow in torrents
with hands like ham bones: by now
I knew I couldn't tame it by myself.

That autumn, I sat on a bed while my maid
tried to groom it. *Does it hurt?* she asked,
as the auburn itself fell like a curtain
over any other possibilities my life held;
she tilted her head and pulled, spilling
a ginger snakeskin over my face and forearms.

In winter, roasting chestnuts, I was caught
in the blaze, my dress became flames,
my maid grabbed the inferno and tried
to brush it out; a jigsaw of shapes held us firmly
in place while in one corner, just in the picture,
a dab of dappled pearl.

Sur Le Pont Des Arts

He's looking at a painting of a river and trees,
houses roughly charcoaled in against a foggy smudge,
a foreground blob that could be a terrier's shadow

or a black hole of invisible light, dark matter
sucking viewers into the artist's untidy mind,
showing them the dissatisfied wife left clearing plates

after a silent Sunday lunch, the son who bores him,
the treasured daughter who ran off to the Pyrenees
with a specialist in sustainable energy

who builds houses out of cartons and solar panels,
where rotas of guests are needed so that they can pee
frequently in order to keep the bathroom lights on.

He's looking at a painting of a river and trees
and thinking about his mistress whom he hasn't seen
for three weeks because she's gone to stay with a sister

he knows she's just invented; now he's thinking about
his new hat, a smart homburg, and how superior
it is to the artist's floppy hat which is hiding,

probably, a mess of impasto passing for brains;
he's thinking of the terrier, who has just caught up
and is now regarding him with small, adoring eyes.

He's thinking it costs him more to feed the terrier
than buying the new homburgs he prefers to his wife.
He's thinking his mistress is a liar, the artist

is an impostor, the artist's wife and son should leave,
the artist's daughter and her husband are complete fakes
and that his own wife is less attractive than a hat.

He's thinking that his terrier is an expensive
excrescence; in fact, he's wishing he was someone else.
He's looking at a painting of a river and trees.

Those Birds Fly Well Which Have Little Flesh

Although it is not in the rules,
she tests herself, leaving the bread
and cheese untouched until her maid
takes it away; and the more she hungers
the more she has to test herself

she is not allowed to beat herself,
to flail herself with nettles
or hedgehog skins – the abbot forbids it

she is not allowed to cut herself,
but she can force herself to lie
on stones until the imprint on her body
is like a nail in her side

she can force herself to sit, undressed
under the window on winter's nights
until her bones groan with cold –

if she doesn't eat, her body will remain
pure and empty to receive the sacrament

the wafer is like honesty, a paper moon,
and she is a fledgling stretching up its beak
to take the gift, turning the web of her blood to silver:
her flesh thin as air.

Fathom

My face
is changing again

I caught it in a different light
yesterday

the flaky grey
of ocean-going
tankers

my face has turned
to someone else's

inside the inside
of the ocean, fish are hanging
cuttle-coloured

they sway, silent
not even a rattle of bones

and the dead stir in us too,
coming as they do from the weight
of darkness

they want our breath

want to tunnel out of us,
force apart our gullets,
appear stark-white

and raving at daylight

one more moment
they plead
just one more.

They Want Our Breath

We think we know that space is silent,
only the words of astronauts reach us
as they stumble as if through water to place
flags while all the time light is escaping
faster than the fastest sandstorm.

Here, the light is full of water, a membrane
of unshed rain, the sky a cheap pendant
you might wear round your neck for love,
the weight of it against your skin, as we,
stumbling home from the fair that time, felt
something pressing on us, invisible, silent:
the moon inside us, using up our breath.

Something Pressing

Summer comes, soft-footed to the doorway,
slips over the sill, threadless and shining,
filling us again with the old yearning,
making us want to skip work for the day:

high in the Altai, Umai shakes her grey
tattooed leather free from ice, and turning
in her grave gives off a smell of burning.
Kali is also on the move, they say:

meanwhile, on Jupiter, the mean wind speed
is three hundred and thirty miles an hour –
a storm the size of Earth which shows up red

on NASA's screens: and, far from Ganymede,
Callisto, the most similar to our
own life-giving planet, is (already) dead.

Prospects

We lay, a dormitory of ten year olds, deciding
which death would be preferable:

Burning from the feet up like Saint Joan
would be worst, someone suggested.
You'd faint before it got too bad – the sturdy girl
cut out to be a nurse assured us.

Yet drowning would be just as horrible
we knew from when we held our breaths
in swimming, buoyant underwater on our silver strings
of seed pearl bubbles.

Worst of all, perhaps, a Viking burial –
scratching at rock until the air went
and us, with our unused breasts and wombs,
buried screaming with the old, dead king.

Aubade

I think of bread and butter sliced thin;
a brown egg, smooth as a knuckle;
a cup of milk, slightly warmed
already forming a brave, new skin.

Then later, chocolates, sweet wine,
maraschino cherries shiny in syrup
reflecting panes of brightness; cream
whipped to an adolescent frenzy.

But, lying here with you, the dawning light
seems, so far, painless. I wait for you to wake
with appetite refreshed by sleep, knowing
what you enjoy most is my hunger.

Baboushka

i.m. Emily Maud Kent 1878-1970

Wherever the Trans-Siberian Express stops
there they are in their boots and headscarves
like shadow puppets against a pliant screen
of thousand-mile birch forests, pushed on
from the wings with trugs of home-made pies,
cold beer and chocolate to sell to travellers.

And the old woman on Komsomol Avenue
bent double by the weight of her shopping
scuttling along the tracks of the trolley bus –
she looked like one of those matryoshkas
they sell for 200 roubles in Arbutt Street
that get smaller and smaller as if receding

into history where small girls help collect
dewberries at their dachas: all that jam-making
for a teaspoonful of sweetness – these children
are brought up on grandmothers' sayings:
lie down with a dog, you'll get up with fleas,
the best way to get rid of work is to do it –

whatever else, Baboushka knows best, there's
comfort in that: just as my own grandmother told
the weather from a feeling in her bones, struggled
with us to the 'gods' at the Old Vic and Aldwych
to give us a taste of Shakespeare, gave herself
half portions so our plates could be full.

Russian Square

for Natasha Dubrovina

Friends told me it was a cleaning woman
who found Pushkin's statue, face down
in the mud in a frock-coat of leaves, red
and yellow with tongues of fire in them:

apparently, she tried to clean him up,
felt it was wrong to leave him, poor man,
but no-one would help – his sort of thinking
wasn't wanted any more, it was about
the same time they started to arrest books.

At last they've reinstated him on his plinth
and made his stories into wrought-iron
wreaths in Pushkin Square, so students
meeting at the benches for coffee can say
once more *Pushkin is everything!*

PETER MCDONALD

Peter McDonald was born in Belfast in 1962. He has published four volumes of poetry, most recently *The House of Clay* (2007), and has written three critical books, including *Serious Poetry: Form and Authority from Yeats to Hill* (2002), as well as editing Louis MacNeice's *Collected Poems* (2007). His next book of poetry will appear in 2011, and he is now editing W.B. Yeats' *Complete Poems* for Longman. He has taught at the Universities of Cambridge and Bristol, and since 1999 he has been Christopher Tower Student and Tutor in Poetry in the English Languages at Christ Church, Oxford. (Photo courtesy of Jemimah Kuhfield.)

The Scald

Half-way up, on the inside, here,
of my right forearm, is the scald:
a whitish outline like a mended tear
in skin that is thirty years healed
– or more than thirty, as it must be –
and was my wrist, the time I scaled
the kitchen table, when a pot of tea
came down; the burn smacked first, then held

and held on while the heat pressed hard
but where, now, you can touch, and touch again,
where you can push into the soft skin
and put your finger on this pucker-scarred
ragged circle the size, say, of a coin,
then take your lips and touch them to the scald.

Quis Separabit

A drive along Belfast's eastern strip
on the home leg of an airport run
at lunchtime, and in blinding rain:
the windscreen's simple weep and wipe,

the roads, the houses, the estates,
all blurred and darkened, out of shape.
The rain, the steady wipe and weep,
brings half in focus, then distorts

Dundonald, and high Castlereagh,
traffic in its long runs below,
with Stormont always just in view
– a smudge of white, of white and grey –

and then the Braniel's show of flags:
as I speed past, I leave behind
an Ulster flag, Ulster's red hand
drenched up there as it slaps and flaps,

beside it – clear as day – the Star
of David, staunch beneath black skies,
flown in defiance where it flies
glaring into the backward mirror,

surviving as one mote of white
lodged like a flaw behind the eyes –
white edged with blue. The message is
a downright question: who will part

blood from blood, and who desert us,
daring to stand here, while we stand?
The road loops back, and has no end.
Here we remain, and who shall part us?

The Blood-Bruise

I worked against it all that afternoon,
the racing bindweed, or convolvulus,
that had gone unchecked, it seemed, by anyone
for weeks, and now made its calamitous
faces everywhere: those deathly-delicate
trompettes, and their lime-white
mouths that opened up, and opened again,
in silent and proliferating forms
strung along cords I had to bundle down
and gather up as tangles in my arms.

I stooped in to the stricken rosebushes
where they had all but given up the ghost
so deeply had the bindweed's ropes and lashes
become involved, and so nearly had they lost
the plot to its inveigling flowers and leaves;
as thorns plucked at my sleeves
I hauled in slippery tendrils by the yard
until my arms could hold no more, my arms
that, now I looked, had been scrabbed and scarred
where they and the sharp roses came to terms.

What I saw then, when I saw you suddenly,
knocked me off-kilter, like a freak shot
or a punch from nowhere, making light of me:
it wasn't even your face at first, and not
your blue-green eyes as they took in my alarm,
but the blood-bruise on your arm
where the skin was softest; where, as I looked,
I almost tracked the course a vein might run
minutely under my fingers; where they unhooked
and undid you, when all of their work was done.

The Thread

How slightly, twenty years ago,
I managed to construe the girl
I met three times, or twice, then so
awkwardly flirted with, by proxy,
dispatching printed poems of mine
whose frail and thin-spun lines
took scarcely any weight (I see
that much), carried no weight at all.

In a bored moment, by sheer chance,
news of her death crosses my eyes,
and minutes pass while I realize
that now, at this far distance,
I can't so much as picture her,
feeling for the least snag or pull
in a line that's barely visible,
and slighter than a thread of hair.

The Neighbours

In the single-bedroom flat I used to cry the night through
as my mother walked the floor with me, rocked me and fed me
past the small, insensible hours, not to wake the neighbours;
though often upstairs there might be half the Group Theatre
going till daybreak – a tiny, bohemian airpocket:
Jimmy Ellis (in the Group, before *Z Cars*), or Mary O'Malley,
and over from next door, next door but one maybe, George
McCann, Mercy Hunter, John Boyd and the BBC,
talking politics or shop, intrigue or gossip the night through:

but perhaps on this occasion there's only the baby
cutting in and out of silence in a high spare room
where the McCanns have just lodged their visiting poet
who by noon will cross from The Elbow Room to the studios
in Ormeau Avenue, and deliver his talk, unscripted,
on 'Childhood Memories'; whose sleep now, if sleep it is,
remains unbroken through the small, insensible hours
between the whiskey nightcap and a breakfast of whiskey.

The Bees

I

When the last of the sunlight goes,
and shadows stretching from the shade
of trees and bushes, long hedgerows,
join up together to invade
wild grasses and the flat pasture,
turning from shadows into night,
then the bees, scattered far and near,
take notice, and start on their flight
back to those walls and roofs they know,
beehives where their small bodies rest
between the dark and dawn; they go
over the threshold, noisy, fast,
massing in hundreds at the doors,
and pour past into their close cells,
cramming chambers and corridors
while the last of the daylight fails:
sleep silences the working hive
and leaves it quiet as the grave.

II

For bees put no trust in the sky
when storms come up with an east wind,
and seldom venture far away
from their stations when downpours impend:
instead, they draw the water off
and stick close to their city walls
where any flights they take are brief;
as the wind blows and the rain falls
they steady themselves through turbulence
by taking with them little stones
(as frail boats, faced with violence
of gales and tides, take ballast on),
and hold their given course along
the clouds, balanced, and balancing.

III

A wonder, how they reproduce:
without courtship, or lovemaking,
without letting their hearts unloose
nerves and sinews like so much string,
without the agony of birth,
they gather offspring from the leaves
and softer herbs, draw with each breath
pollen and children for the hives,
providing themselves with a fresh
ruler, and tiny citizens,
to take the place of some who crash
against the earth, onto hard stones,
brought level by their single love
for flowers, and honey-vintages
(the glorious legacy they leave
behind them, in trust for the ages),
although the time that waits for them
is short enough, and not beyond
a seventh summer; yet the same
nation and race will soldier on,
deathless in spite of time's attacks,
in cells and palaces of wax.

IV

All of these things have given pause
to the bees' watchers and guardians
whenever they ascribe the cause
to some influx, some influence
over and above the natural,
an exhalation from beyond
or an element more ethereal
than air itself – maybe the mind
of God, that strengthens as it runs
in earth and sky, or turns in deep
acres of churning oceans,
in herds of cattle, flocks of sheep,
the wild beasts and the harmless beasts,
in life that feels along a thread
from its first moment to the last,
finishing where it all started,
and never reaching a true end:
this keeps the bees away from death
when, at the last, they all ascend
into the skies they lived beneath,
to fly between undarkened spheres
in heaven, and the many stars.

– from Virgil, Georgics, *Book IV*

The Weather

Weightless to me, the heavy leaves
on a sumach drag down their long stems
ready to fall, and spend their lives
on one inflamed, extravagant
display, when light like the rain teems
over and through them; ruined, pendent,
parading every colour of fire
on a cold day at the edge of winter.

They are like the generations of man
of course, and we knew that; we knew
everything pretty much in advance
about this weather: light like the rain,
the red-gold and the gold tattoo
that dying things can print on ruin
(no ruin, in fact, except their own),
flaring up even as they go down.

The sunshine makes reds virulent
and yellows vibrant with decay;
it's not surprise, more like assent
when they fall, when I let them fall,
to what is fated, in its way,
of which this rain-cleared light makes little,
meaning the day can gleam, can glow:
and not a bad day, as days go.

JILL MCDONOUGH

Jill McDonough has been teaching college English courses in Massachusetts prisons since 1999. A graduate of Boston University's Creative Writing program, her poems appear in the *Threepenny Review, Poetry*, the *New Republic*, and *Slate*. Published 2008, *Habeas Corpus*, her first book of poems, is fifty sonnets about executions in American history from 1608 to 2005. Her awards include a Pushcart Prize and fellowships from the NEA, the Fine Arts Work Center, Stanford's Stegner Program, and the Cullman Center for Scholars and Writers. She is a 2010 Witter Bynner Fellow at the Library of Congress. (Photo courtesy of Robert Maloney.)

June 4, 1715: Margaret Gaulacher

Boston, Massachusetts

The news that week includes a *lyoness*
displayed, attacking *Fowls* and *Catts*. They watched
her feeding time, remarked on her *merciless*
cruelty. Meanwhile, Cotton Mather preached
against *Hard-hearted Sinners*, and *Hardness of Heart*.
He helped with her confession, which reflects
on attempts to destroy her unborn child, a part
of her *Wicked* crime, completed through *Neglect*.
Now hers is a *Stony Heart, of Flint*. *Ah! Poor*
Margaret, behold: the congregation calls
on your *wondrous Industry, Agony,* your death four
days off. Pray for a *Clean, and a Soft Heart*; don't fall
from this fresh gallows to *the Mouths of Dragons,*
unconcerned, *adamant, so little broken*.

October 21, 1773: Levi Ames

Boston, Massachusetts

My first thefts were small. A couple of eggs, and then
a jack-knife. After that some chalk. A fair
piece of broadcloth, a silver spoon and ten
or eleven dollars from Mr. Symond. A pair
of silver buckles, twelve tea-spoons, silk mitts.

He asks the preacher for this psalm: My heart
is smitten, and withered like grass, so I forget
to eat my bread, &c. *My time is so short.*

He reads Ezekiel: A new heart will
I give you, &c. For my heart was bad,
bad indeed. At the gallows he asked if the souls
of the wicked, at death, would appear before our God
or immediately pass to Hell, and wait their doom.

Soon, dear sir, I shall know more than you.

October 8, 1789: Rachel Wall

Boston, Massachusetts

The woodcut illustrating *Life, Last Words*
and Dying CONFESSION, of RACHEL WALL: a child's
dark awkward house, a ladder slanting toward
three figures, hanging above the crowd that piled
onto cobbles to watch three robbers hang,
and one a woman. The picture's clumsy. Still,
her petticoats, small bodice are portrayed
in detail. She said she never robbed that girl,
but did admit that she deserved to die:
the gold she stole from *under the captain's head,*
asleep at *Long-Wharf. Sabbath-breaking*. The lie
that got another woman whipped in her stead:

I declare the crippled Dorothy Horn
innocent of the theft at Mr. Vaughn's

July 9, 1819: Rose Butler

Potter's Field, New York, New York

To be sent in a cart to State Prison, to climb the stairs
to the attic, where the women are kept, and left
there, left in that close heat with strangers, their
children, their filthy bodies. Charged with theft,
say. Rats. Fleas. Cholera, buckets of shit, and years
spent fighting, trapped there, forgotten till you died.

The preacher visits her holding cell and swears
she's *sure to go to hell*. The Sheriff's kind:
gives her an orange, a ride in a coach, at last,
to the gallows. She'd dreaded a cart. They tie black bows
at her feet and neck, tie her white shroud, and ask
Would you rather go to the State Prison, Rose?

Just curious. *She stood like a lamb*, still, *dumb*.
She thought of the cart. *No. I had rather be hung.*

April 22, 1831: Charles Gibbs

Ellis Island, New York

The court's death sentence for his piracy
and murders said it should be public, by hanging,
and then went further: his body, they decreed,
would go *to the College* to be dissected. Waiting
to die, he was heartened to hear of an attempt
to make hanging more certain, *painless*, quick
by slinging them up, instead of dropping them.
Five fifty-six pound weights, rope one inch thick,
two *pulleys, scaffold thirteen feet from the earth.*
Gibbs called the doctor, asked *in a lowered tone*
could he die easier by holding his breath
or breathing out? Perhaps *the latter mode.*
Rope cut, he was *drawn up* but struggled, freed
his hands and tore at the hood, dying to breathe.

June 19, 1953: Julius and Ethel Rosenberg

Ossining, New York

Electrocution set for eight p.m.
Two hours before they took him to be prepped
the matrons asked her if she'd like to see him;
the warden said that they could take some steps
to let them talk. A screen of metal mesh
between two wooden chairs outside her cell.
Romantic. Pyramus and Thisbe, rushed
in writing letters to their kids, to tell
them *Remember: we were innocent, and could*
not wrong our conscience. Now we press you close
and kiss you with all our strength. Before they stood
to go he kissed two fingers, pressed them both
against the screen, to hers: first white, then red.
Their final touch, through screen. So hard they bled.

August 9, 2000: Brian Roberson

Huntsville, Texas

On a night of *drinking, smoking PCP*
mixed with formaldehyde, he stabbed his neighbors,
a white couple, and killed them. He said he believed
he did it, but couldn't imagine why, since *they were*
the nicest people on the block.
                                                    His father
was stabbed to death by a white junkie when Brian
was ten: not a mitigating factor
but a motive, according to the court. So *why*
is it that white man who murdered my husband got
thirteen years? Brian's mother asked.
                                                    His last
words were for *racist white folks, black folks who hate*
themselves, the words of my famous brother Nat
Turner: y'all kiss my black ass. Smiling, he died,
and they cleared the room for the second injection that night.

August 9, 2000: Oliver Cruz

Hunstville, Texas

He *raped* Kelly Donovan, *stabbed her 20 times*
and *left her body alongside the road*. The state
said *he may not be very smart,* but tried
this out: *it makes him more dangerous*. He made

some progress, his years in prison: *I can write*
a letter, a half a page. He didn't know
what *retarded* meant. When he went to the chamber to die,
sobbing, teary-eyed, he said *Take me home,*
Jesus. I'm sorry. When there's only one
lethal injection a night, it's at six, but Cruz
went half an hour after Roberson.
The same chamber, same gurney, but they used

new sheets, needles, and tubing for each one.
Five minutes after strapping in Cruz they were done.

Runaway

1728 Advertisement for the Recovery of an Indian Servant

I'll miss her smoky cooking, beans
in molasses, coffee with cream. Warm
mornings, her clean kitchen. Soapy streams
of fresh-pumped water on her arms.
Her *Narrow Stript pink Cherredary*
Goun turn'd up with a little flour'd
red & white Callico. Contrary,
very pretty. And vain. Spent hours
at her sewing. Everything in a birch
bark basket. Clean. She had a pretty
body, worked hard in the kitchen, stitched
quick, tidy stitches. Used too little
nutmeg, too much mace. In *A stript*
Homespun Quilted Petticoat, plain
muslin Apron. She loved the ripe
pears from the pear tree, glazed with rain.
Her hair in tidy plaits: *plain Pinners*
& a red & white flower'd knot.

Come back, beloved. Oils, paper,
whatever you lack. An apricot
tree, blue ribbons. A necklace to match
your *green Stone Earrings*. A dozen pairs
of *White Cotton Stockings,* a latch
for your door, lace, linen aprons to wear
if you'd come back to Pinckney Street,
this narrow brick house with its new
porch. Over the cobbled pavers. Neat
in your *Leather heel'd Wooden Shoes*.

Ontogeny Recapitulates Phylogeny

My young parents, telling
us stories about biology
class, MacMurray, class
of '64, the year
my mother wore the turquoise
leather mini-skirt we knew
from the dress-up box, tossed
in with blue velvet, blue tulle, tasseled
white leather majorette boots, baton,
poodle-embroidered circle
skirts straight out of *Happy*
Days. We wore them
with gramma's veiled and feathered
hats, mom's frosted wig, imagined
the glamour of prom, or college, getting
married, having babies, growing up.
At the reunion, Professor Whatsisname
remembered my dad was the best
in their class, looked at my mother's legs
before saying, warmly, *Oh, yes, you*
sat in front. Ontogeny recapitulates
phylogeny, my parents recited,
remembering when they were
young and wrote this stuff
in notebooks, had notebooks,
memorized what dead men
said. When we asked what
it meant, they struggled, laughing, easily
distracted: dinosaurs, walking fish,
tadpole-looking embyros
growing into baby girls. We thought
we'd study it in college, but by the time
we got to college, nobody wrote it down
in notebooks. Ontogeny recapitulates
phylogeny: outdated as saddle

shoes, veiled hats, monkeys'
uncles, *Inherit the Wind*.

PATRICK MCGUINNESS

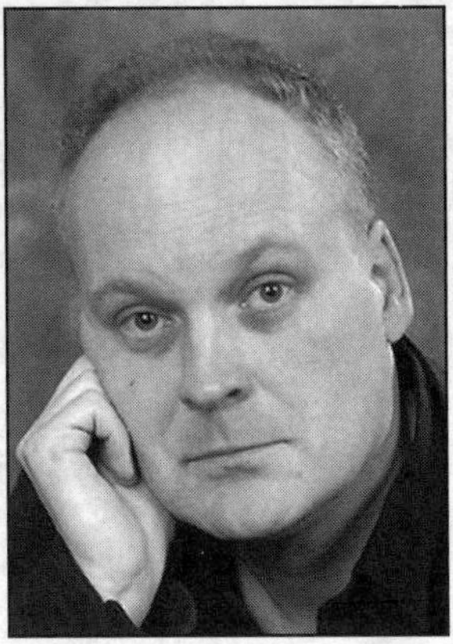

Patrick McGuinness was born in 1968 in Tunisia of Belgian and Anglo-Irish parents. His books of poetry include *The Canals of Mars* (2004), *19th Century Blues* (2007) and *Jilted City* (2010). His translation of Mallarmé's *For Anatole's Tomb* appeared in 2004, and his novel, *The Last Hundred Days,* about the fall of the Ceausescu régime in Romania, will appear in 2011. He teaches French and Comparative Literature at St. Anne's College, Oxford, and lives in Caernarfon, Wales. (Photo courtesy of Douglas Gowan.)

from *Blue Guide*

I – *Gare du Nord*

Arriving is like walking in on someone else's divorce
proceedings: Belgium-wide, the Balkans, their weather,
their slowly fissuring statelets ripening into crisis,
averted crisis, crisis. There are no last straws;
that's a law we Belgians learned too late; some of us

not at all. The rain falling slantwise over *Gare du Nord*:
Brussels composing its island weather, *Symphony*
in grey major, the nineteenth century still shaking
on the rails, the twentieth a late train.

II - *Gare Centrale*

I had it for a moment, quick as the clash of two winds on a rooftop:
the smell of barley, hops, fresh diesel and its negative – used air;
then *Belga* smoke over the exhalations of the *waffel*-stand:

This feeling of penetrating misery is sponsored by Brussels
City Council in association with SNCB announced a voice
in white over the station Tannoy. I filed this one away between

two stops, between *Bruxelles-Nord* and *Bruxelles-*
Midi, between the word *départ*, so definitive and final,
and the word *partance*, an ongoing going, a leaving

still entangled in itself years later like the sound of a train
turning the corner, its siren coiled around the echo of the last to go
and the tunnel taking a moulding of our departures.

III - *Gare du Midi*

Noon, the day's South Pole. On separate trains again:
window to window, each of us learns our sense
of movement from the way the other pulls away.

IV - *Quartier-Léopold*

Colonial moss and plumes of baroque fern ...
a station like a mouldy cake layered for a forgotten
coronation: icing stucco, pillars of sponge,

then a heart of darkness where the train stops,
a spasm in the network: the doors stay closed,
and the windows bead with tropical damp.

A moment in the striplit shadows, *Gare de Léopoldville,*
then we ease back into Belgium, a barge
sliding through diamond-studded blood and water.

V – *Schuman*

(The other Robert Schuman, one *n*, this one
so anonymous they named a station after him
where it's dark enough to cultivate endives,

breed bats and harvest mushrooms,
where the only music is piped like chloroform
from unseen speakers into Euroland's conditioned air.)

The Age of the Empty Chair

In Monet's *The Beach at Trouville,* it is week one of the Franco-Prussian war.
The chair lodges in the sand between two women. One reads, the other

points her face at the emptying beach. The chair belongs to no-one,
it is a found chair, a *trouvaille,* and there is never one chair too many

but one sitter too few. A flag rigid on its pole indicates
a swelling in the air, or something stronger, and the rent waves,

delicate turmoils of spume and lace, are distant cousins of the revolution
bound into the ebb and flow it breaks free of, then breaks back into.

There is sand in the paint; the place is mixed into its making
and even the brushstrokes replicate the water's peaks as they take

the light: roves pell-mell across a city skyline, flashpoints in the sun.
The chair suggests all that can be suggested about change, but it remains

apart from it: the way a sail suggests the wind, the way a shell holds
a recording of the waves even as the waves turn around it.

Black Box

Every crashed marriage has its black box, the blow-
by-blow account of what went wrong and how,
the crescendo of mistakes that peaks, is for an instant
quiet on its crest of trauma, then drowns itself and us

in a cascade of static. The black box is what survives;
anthracite gleaming in the wreckage where, preserved in angers,
the voices that it holds replay their lifetime of last moments
and speak of how, until the very end, it might have been

so different; and how, right from the start, they knew it never would.

The Museum of Archaeology

Proust's theory, one we disbelieve
despite our lives' daily demonstration of its truth,
is that what survives of us
is what was least intended to go on after.

The museums know that, with their shelves
of fluent trivia: whole civilizations summoned up
by beaten gold that's finer than skin, shards
of pot whose brokenness now renders them unbreakable,

sky-blue glass blown by one whose breath survives only
in the bubbles that were caught there, sculpted now
as tiny voids around which our idea of life beads
because there's nothing to it but what holds it in:

a see-through brittle shell of light around what only
looks like nothing. It's the nearest *we*'ll get to pure form,
to seeing it I mean, to time without the clock,
the river without the bank, that point when either

all is form or there's no such thing; in other words,
when form is most itself, both essence and tautology.
Proust knew it, whose every microsmos of a sentence
could have stood alone, the novel's DNA, the pinhead-dance

of all the world's complexity and ours in face of it;
and yet who needed the whole three thousand pages too,
to build up what had to be reduced.

from *The Canals of Mars*

Belgitude

I spent autumn learning about autumn,
that its unmistakable confusion about what it was
was what made it what it was. So with Belgium.
It was the first post-national state; wars
came there to be fought, got tired and moved on.
Surveys showed that most Belgians questioned

would have preferred to be from somewhere else:
truly this was home, I thought, all the more
so as home had been a drain on my awareness,
took a little more of me away from me each year.
I came to it side-on, as one climbs into a moving bus;
discovered the world was a small town, or

at any rate vice versa. Soon I learned
to keep my mouth shut in two languages;
I called home on lobster telephones
in a hail of bowler hats. Trains ran on time,
travelling micro-distances in decades.
After a while I fitted in, by looking out of place,

swept into a street-long tidal wave of curtain lace.

Father and Son

in memory of my father, and in welcome to my son

In the wings there is one who waits to go on,
and another, his scene run, who waits to go.
I would like to think they met; if not here
then like crossed letters touching in the dark;

the blank page and the turned page,
the first and the last, shadows folding
over and across me, in whom they're bound.

ANDREW MCNEILLIE

Andrew McNeillie is a Professor of English at Exeter University, having previously been Literature Editor at Oxford University Press. His latest volume of poems, *In Mortal Memory,* was published this year. In addition to four volumes of verse, he is the author of a memoir, *An Aran Keening* (2001), and its belated prequel, *Once* (2009). He is also the founding editor of the literary magazine *Archipelago,* from Clutag Press, which also publishes poetry, including work by Geoffrey Hill, in the booklet *A Treatise of Civil Power* (2005) and the CD *Poetry Reading, Oxford, 1st February 2006*. (Photo courtesy of Jemimah Kuhfield.)

In the Wilderness

Who was I in the stranger's guise
and who were they in theirs?
I went among them, the latest of my kind,
while they were first forever to my mind.
And life itself so passing strange
that I had time for nothing else
and time I had as never since.
All spent to show what neither could
know or guess would come to pass,
word for word, the test of time.

Losings

These findings brought home,
objects of no use, unless to hold
a page against a draft or decorate
a sill or hearth, give weight,
featherweight even to weightlessness.
I should call them losings
even as they take hold on routine.

As if heard but not seen,
their presences in what proportion
absences? Tap the barometer
to know, from one day to another.
The heart's variable weather
begins with such things
once living, and unseen.

Aran Keening

i.m. Tom Hernon d. 17 November aet 87

My friend sent me a photo of his coffin
lying in state at Onacht, with his cap on,
... People from 'the islands' and
two sisters from America, the whole island,
came to pay their last respects.
I should have joined them, sent regrets?
But they barely waited and he was in
the airy ground, the moment gone.
I can see them though, in that wake of rain
and sudden break and gash of sun
opened to order, over the graveyard,
and the 'huge' crowd of mourners gathered
above the bay at Cill Mhuirbigh where
the hero of my hour lived and died.
I was two weeks in at this anniversary,
my forty-first, a Tuesday to the day
he breathed his last: a 'dole-day', for irony.
His only holiday, his mother said.

The Lively Lady

lost with all hands 1 March 1982

It's a downhill struggle, in an ocean of losses,
A shoreline of cobble and pebble and the sea's
hearthstone, swept after the tide-blaze, and spark
of wader-flight, starlight in the quick dark,
their calling like my own. Nothing changes?
That bay of 'silver sand' and marram, its embrace,
its waiting. I could settle for it were I able
to sail into view and put in there for a while
for the boys to get a meal just up the hill.

A Waulking Dream

Six young girls shrink the cloth –
draw breath, draw breath –
singing slowly to begin with
then livelier with a tightening song,
next a stretching, followed by folding,
and never a word of their dreaming.

Wallflower

I never wanted to, but put me through it
I did, imagining my shyness to be
undecided, and sometimes finding pity.
But I look askance at them now and all that
marriage has entailed, for those forward
blooms who couldn't bear to be ignored.

Ruin

The Gallic word RUIN
translates as DESIRES.
The eye wanders here
and the mind wonders
where these two meet
at each other's wake.

Rush Light

Energy-saver, poring dimly over print,
consider how your light is spent
and think before it is too late
how once again to serve the State
the young grow up illiterate.

The Journey

I came back and stayed on
my head turned by a girl
and what I didn't know
about the place I was in.

Under the same streeling light
habitual to my mind, between
sea and mountain, I taught
myself another lesson.

How the familiar opens out.
How all horizons meet
under you, invisibly,
if you pause to think.

As prompted this morning
waiting at the quay for the visitors,
their cameras already busy
as they come ashore.

Elegy

I want to put you out to grass, set
you aside, and leave you fallow.

For you to winter an aeon or two
And watch time pass without regret.

LUCY NEWLYN

Lucy Newlyn is a Professor of English Language and Literature at Oxford University, and a Fellow and Tutor in English at St Edmund Hall. She has published widely on English Romantic literature, including three books with Oxford University Press and the *Cambridge Companion to Coleridge*. Her book *Reading, Writing, and Romanticism: The Anxiety of Reception* won the British Academy's Rose Mary Crawshay prize in 2001. She is currently editing a selection of Edward Thomas's prose. Her first collection of poems, *Ginnel,* was published by Oxford*Poets*/Carcanet in 2005. Further poems selected here also first appeared in *Oxford Magazine*. (Photo courtesy of Emma Slater.)

Washing-Day

That great white sheet on the line
is big-bellied with buffeting wind,
and the woman is pegging it
with hands bent on pummelling bread.

The big-bellied woman is beaten
by the wind, and blown about
in the billowing sheet. But her feet
are bound to the blashy ground,

and her hands bent on pummelling
move fast, as the wind dries the sheet.
The thoughts of the woman
are big-bellied with child and bread

like the sheet in the buffeting wind:
she'll have the sheet pegged and dried
in the wind before the soot darkens it;
then she'll pummel the bread for the child.

I'm pegging my thoughts on the line
in the buffeting wind. I'm the wind
billowing thoughts, and they're blown
about like the great white sheet.

I'm the child in the big-bellied woman.
My hands pummel her belly as she pegs
the sheet. I'm the yeast in the bread,
and the blashy ground at her feet.

So we rub along together, the woman,
the wind, and the child: forever bent
on beating the soot, and drying the sheet,
so the bread can be pummelled, and rise.

Walls

for the Metcalfes of Appersett

I love the curt sounds of the vowels –
the way they hold back and stay put
like through-stones in wind-bitten walls:
'appen, mucky, luv, thissen, mek, nowt.
The consonants sturdy as footings
or knobbly as topstones, with a shut
sound – *taffled, snicket, sneck, tekken* –
to keep the sheep in and the gales out.
All the words rough and showing
their edges, with glottal stops as packers:
Ah s'll be dahn on mi nogs ower lang
bah missen in t' claggy muck and watter.
And the whole fabric holding together
without mortar against age and weather.

Crossing the Ridge

The longest ginnel I know
moves across the map
like two big tacking-stitches
or the broken furrow of a plough.

It starts where the bluebells grow
under the oaks in Batty's wood
and climbs in a deep groove
between tall houses, over the brow

of the Ridge to the far side,
where it blanks out
on Cumberland Road in brightness:
empty, un-selving, wide.

Then it rallies; and down –
diagonally left and down –
it delves like something
dark and purposive, into town.

Thirty years since I walked here,
and not a stone changed.
Only a moment's hesitation
after climbing, as I stand where

the ginnel closes on light
and opens on darkness –
caught in the bright hiatus,
a thief in the night.

A Rebellion

in memory of JFW

He admired the long, low lines,
the rectangular, end-stopped blocks
running exactly parallel with the spaces

and broken only in the middle, with nothing
to interrupt the eye's steady passage
from opening to opening.

It was all urbanity and cool abstraction –
a Scandinavian utopia of vast skies,
clear vanishing-points, clean edges.

But none of this satisfied.

Was it mischief, or simply a longing
that made him plant seeds
in-between,

so that, over the years,
the roots worked their way
under?

As the rectangles loosened,
they lost their neat alignments,
and a softness came

in waves
and climbing, arching green.

Self-seeding, proliferating,
a thicket of unruly buddleias
sported their plumes near his window –

attracting, in August,
peacocks, red admirals, tortoiseshells,
fritillaries, and (once in a while)

a small white.

The Swallows

for Pamela

The swallows come to the sitting room window as if wishing to build but I am afraid they will not have courage for it, but I believe they will build at my room window. They twitter & make a bustle & a little cheerful song hanging against the panes of glass, with their soft white bellies close to the glass & their forked fish-like tails. They swim round & round & again they come.

– Dorothy Wordsworth, *Grasmere Journal,* June 16, 1802)

What if they nested here, so close
we could almost touch,
and sense each other listening?

She settles, but they circle again
and again, the rushing bubble of song
submerged by flap and wash of wings.

Magnified, they hang, bellies
pressed against the pane,
fins waving, bills silently opening.

Their eyes are aeons deep and away,
but looking in.
She's absorbed,
suspended in air, glass, water.

Something is stirring inside,
and they keep bumping, bumping
their soft white bellies up against my skin.

Found

For too long the sky has bullied
the hills into submission.

Hindscarth, Dale Head, Robinson
lie sunk under a sodden weight of cloud,

their dark backs bowed and hidden.
Now, in sudden folds that heave

and shudder, chop and start,
the sullen waves are driven

across a lake recalcitrant
and leaden

as the rough, black, heart-shaped stone
she lugged home unbidden.

French Windows

It all followed as a matter of course
after the side of the house
was opened up, no-one noticing at first

the train of consequences
which slipped one after the other
through French windows latticing the garden.

*

Silt of sunshine, tree dapple, sky's clarities
in glass, and the painting of walls
in various shades of sage, leaf, grass, apple.

A lifted carpet; the laying bare
and smoothing-down of a wooden floor.
A rug paved in warm earth colours.

The slow creeping over mantels and tables
of house plants. Shiver of leaf-shadow
and leaf shape, each side of windows.

*

Days lengthening, and the house hinged
on one side like a doll's, wide open
to the summer's murmurings:

laughter, to and fro of children;
smells of cooking along the breathing edges
of gardens. Tables and chairs spreading

from room to patio. Twist and flutter of birds
in a mirror, the tiny white thread of a plane
crossing the lacquered surface of the piano.

*

All day long, time's seepage between
floorboards. Knots darkening in the wood grain
like eyes. Cracks furring over with leaf spore,

lichen; butterflies folding on cushions,
the garden settling itself quietly into the room,
bringing the sky with it, and all its flitting,

velvety companions. At dusk the soft flap
of moths on light shades, or high up
in corners the webbed skin wings of bats.

*

And all this happening slowly,
as a matter of course, with no one noticing,
till one night coming down

to find the room a garden,
with the trees hushed, and the owls
hooting, and the windows still open.

Jiuzhaigou

In China, one of the many
symbols for longevity is a crane.

There are no cranes wading
the lakes at Jiuzhaigou

where tens of thousands
of people come each day

to photograph water
clearer than any blue.

Nothing stirs on the side
of Yellow Dragon mountain.

No bats fly out of the tall woods,
darker than any silence.

The narrow path circles Swan Lake
without ever touching the water.

You must keep to the path,
directing your gaze

to the smooth azure, where no
goldfish or minnows swim.

At the bottom of Panda Lake,
skeletons of fallen pines

in their hundreds
lie sunk and still.

On a stone near the water's edge,
hope settles,

folds her delicate wings,
and is caught on film.

Anniversary

No snow came soundlessly
on this non day
from nowhere strangely

bringing muffled voices
and treacherous bouquets
draped in cellophane.

How you hated
(freesias the one exception)
these corpses fed on water and aspirin,

roses for visiting
lilies for burying
tulips for remembering:

a good show,
like the see-through coffin
you wore your best velvet in.

All the long morning
was your winding sheet unwinding
your body lifted from linen.

All afternoon
an immense bowl
of empty floodlit now

filling steadily with then
in slow motion
and then again.

BERNARD O'DONOGHUE

Bernard O'Donoghue was born in the north of County Cork in 1945, and he still spends part of the year there. He has lived in England since 1962, and since 1965, in Oxford, where he is now a Fellow in Medieval English at Wadham College. He has published five volumes of poems, with Gallery Press and Chatto and Windus, and his *Selected Poems* was published by Faber and Faber in 2008. He has translated *Sir Gawain and the Green Knight* for Penguin, as well as written critical books on medieval European love poetry and on Seamus Heaney. (Photo courtesy of Cornelia Carson.)

A Nun Takes the Veil

That morning early I ran through briars
To catch the calves that were bound for market.
I stopped the once, to watch the sun
Rising over Doolin across the water.

The calves were tethered outside the house
While I had my breakfast: the last one at home
For forty years. I had what I wanted (they said
I could), so we'd loaf bread and Marie biscuits.

We strung the calves behind the boat,
Me keeping clear to protect my style:
Confirmation suit and my patent sandals.
But I trailed my fingers in the cool green water,

Watching the puffins driving homeward
To their nests on Aran. On the Galway mainland
I tiptoed clear of the cow-dunged slipway
And watched my brothers heaving the calves

As they lost their footing. We went in a trap,
Myself and my mother, and I said goodbye
To my father then. The last I saw of him
Was a hat and jacket and a salley stick,

Driving cattle to Ballyvaughan.
He died (they told me) in the county home,
Asking to see me. But that was later:
As we trotted on through the morning-mist,

I saw a car for the first time ever,
Hardly seeing it before it vanished.
I couldn't believe it, and I stood up looking
To where I could hear its noise departing

But it was only a glimpse. That night in the convent
The sisters fussed me, but I couldn't forget
The morning's vision, and I fell asleep
With the engine humming through the open window.

Nel Mezzo del Cammin

No more overcoats; maybe another suit,
A comb or two, and that's my lot.
So the odd poem (two in a good year)
Won't do to make the kind of edifice
You'd hope to leave. Flush out the fantasy:
The mid-point being passed, the pattern's clear.
This road I had taken for a good byway
Is the main thoroughfare; and even that
Now seems too costly to maintain.
Too many holes to fill; not enough time
To start again. 'I wasn't ready. The sun
Was in my eyes. I thought we weren't counting.'

Soon we'll be counting razorblades and pencils.

O'Regan the Amateur Anatomist

The gander clapped out its flat despair
While O'Regan sawed at its legs with his penknife.
He looked at me with a friendly smile as blood
Dripped in huge, dark drips. I didn't protest
Or flail out at him, but smiled in return,
Knowing what grown-ups do, whatever breeds
About their hearts, is always for the best.
Worms are cold-blooded; babies learn in the night
By being left to cry. Another time (a man
So generous, they said, he'd give you the sweet
From his mouth) he halved a robin with that knife.
Finally, racing his brother back from a funeral
Down a darkening road, he drove his car
Under a lightless lorry, cutting his head off.
I wonder what he thought he was up to then?

The Nuthatch

I couldn't fathom why, one leafless
Cloudcast morning he appeared to me,
Taking time off from his rind-research
To spread his chestnut throat and sing
Outside my window. His woodwind
Stammering exalted every work-day
For weeks after. Only once more
I saw him, quite by chance, among
The crowding leaves. He didn't lift
His head as he pored over his wood-text,
And, ashamed of the binocular intrusion,
Like breath on eggs or love pressed too far,
I'm trying to pretend I never saw him.

The State of the Nation

'The condition upon which God hath given liberty to man is eternal vigilance'
– John Philpot Curran, 1790

Before I fell asleep, I had been reading
How in the Concentration Camps, alongside
The Jewish personal effects, were stored
For future reference gipsies' earrings,
Scarves and the crystal globes in which they saw
The future; and how the Guardia Civil
Swept through Fuente Vaqueros, smashing guitars.

The book was open still when I woke up
At dawn and, not reassured by the May chorus
From the cypresses, ran to the encampment
At the crossroads where slow smoke curled by the sign
'Temporary Dwellings Prohibited.'
Still there; spread in dew along the hedges
Were gossamer and shawls and tea-towels.

A chained dog watched me peering under
The first canvas flap. Empty. The rest the same.
Not a soul in any tent. I straightened up
And listened through the sounds of morning
For voices raised in family rows, or their ponies
Tocking back from venial raids, bringing home
Hay, a clutch of eggs, unminded pullets.

The Iron-Age Boat at Caumatruish

If you doubt, you can put your fingers
In the holes where the oar-pegs went.
If you doubt still, look past its deep mooring
To the mountains that enfold the corrie's
Waterfall of lace through which, they say,
You can see out but not in.
If you doubt that, hear the falcon
Crying down from Gneeves Bog
Cut from the mountain-top. And if you doubt
After all these witnesses, no boat
Dredged back from the dead
Could make you believe.

Vanellus, Vanellus

When I'd forgotten them, you told me how
I saw them in the morning going to school,
Tattering down the sallow sky of winter.
Now I know them well: I see them every mile
By flocks and companies in roadside fields
As I drive onwards through these snowcast days
To sit at your bed evoking them for you.

The Potter's Field

With better luck he might have been a saint
Or, failing that, lived richly on the interest,
Since thirty silver pieces is a lot.
Yet he flung his fortune back on principle
And, weeping, ran away and hanged himself.
Hearing that tale the first time, any child
Might well, until instructed, cry at his fate.

So what made him the byword for a traitor,
Forever gnawed by thin-lipped Dante's Satan?
Observe the lettering above the gate:
'Iscariot's cemetery for foreign nationals.'
Bequests like his win no one love; their need's
Resented, like a prostitute's caress
Consigned by its beneficiary to Hell.

Somewhere near Rockall in the western ocean,
There is a crag that spits the Atlantic's spray
Back in its face. There, once a century,
Judas sits for the night, his lips refleshing
In the wind, craving the beads of water
He sees hang in every purple clapper
Down endless avenues of seaboard fuchsia.

My tears-of-god bloom as red here beside
The Queen Elizabeth and Iceberg roses
As on their native drywall back in Kerry.
The soil's hospitable; the air is delicate.
So I think that now I'm well enough heeled in
To rate a plot inside the graveyard wall,
Escaping Giudecca. Accurséd be his name!

Father Christmas

It was May or June when I first glimpsed him,
Not far away: as ever, out of season.
Either when the twilight thrush proclaims
Unending summer, or when the guilty children
Rummage through dark wardrobes for Christmas parcels,
In he blunders with his awful timing,
Red suit pulled over his dustcoat any old how,
Beard hooked crooked from his ears, and thrusting out
His dread portfolio of unnaturalised Greek terms:
Aorta; cardiac; thrombosis. Or policemen's words
That make it all sound warranted:
Stroke; violent; massive; laboured; and arrest.

St Brigid's Night

The Sacred Heart lamp's dull perpetual ember
glows on a nunlike woman, paintbox-brown
and cruciform from waist to wimple.
Not like the Swedish Venus of her name
whose votives, new Norse raiders come,
nubile from plane and ferry, causing dread
in guileless christians. Yet she too ushers spring,
they say: rousing the dormant sap again,
brushing with dew the rushcross on the lintel.

VIDYAN RAVINTHIRAN

Vidyan Ravinthiran is a graduate student and lecturer at Balliol College, Oxford. His pamphlet, 'At Home or Nowhere', was published in 2008 by Tall Lighthouse. Acknowledgements are made to *Poetry Review, The North* and the *Times Literary Supplement,* in which some of these poems have appeared; other work has been published, or is forthcoming, in *Magma, Ambit, Stand, Horizon Review, The Oxonian Review,* and *Poetry Wales*. He was commended in this year's Bridport Prize and also shortlisted for an Eric Gregory Award in 2009. He has given readings in Oxford, London, Brighton and Reading.

Uncanny Valley

I had been walking further and further into a desert
of yearning silicon – the air shimmered

in oblongs already, you could hear voices
crying out softly

from thousands of viewless windows.
Life without walls – well you need walls,

load-bearing and beautiful, to fix
the windows in, and you know her hair

is never so beautiful as when she's crying out
from the window and letting it down

so you can scamper up. So much hair, so intricately
braided and pinned that its sheer brushfire

exerts little to no pull on the skin of the scalp,
so you could go on climbing forever

toward the mirage crashing and burning in the air
and her entreaties would never be those of pain.

Yin and Yang

Big raindrops topple from the scaffold hatch
outside the Springbok sports bar where we've gone to watch
the third day of the Olympics – while he goes to the bar
I remark to myself their orbit around each other,
how years since that night outside college they began to play
creator and critic, finishing each other's stories or leading them
    astray,
gently deconstructing the anxiety behind the text ,
one drink with the happy couple playing Who's On Next
makes me the third wheel
of Dharma all over again, beyond speech and unreal –
now he's back and in minutes she's on her iPhone™
browsing Snopes for this latest factoid of his – it sounds a bit
mad – that if everyone in China were to jump all as one
then the planet itself would get put out of orbit.

The Elect

The way those who've made it describe how they made it,
with a slight smugness and fondling of the anecdote –
a taxi shared with, a course signed up for, serendipitous,
how like the matchstick girl stood around looking piteous
they were randomly picked up while at work
by the giant hand in the sky which would make
their career; such patterning, such beauty in the world
in which they found their happiness. Such faith in the word
in your ear in a cool alcove – before the party
breaks up, the plates shift, the elect require their mystery
should wall guilt out for good. And their 'just so'
stories – *it just so happened, and I was lucky that, and if it hadn't*
been
for X's generosity, Y's sense of the changing scene,
well I wouldn't be here talking to you now!

Ladies and Germs

When he walks into the room he floats his palm out by his side
following at a distance every contour of the wall – like there's a pelt
of invisible fur over everything he must stroke but with

the back of his hand only. And his right hand always knows
what his left is doing as they wash each other in a complex pro-
    cedure
designed to defer the burden of dirt at several removes from his body

to the tainted taps before the white basin's safely rinsed clean.
He must leap the unidentifiable black smut like char on the landing;
although he doesn't drink he makes outrageous assertions at the bar

like killing newborns is fine as they haven't yet achieved personhood.
His genetic explanation for all human behaviour is apt to degrade
into mere fatalism – the spunky girls he's taken with are invariably
    taken

with his evil for a day or two then fail to grasp the nettle.
Their cleavage disgusts him anyway, an arse re-installed
where society can see it. He likes Duchamp, had six-inch spikes
    and thins

like he wants to disappear entirely. In the future the body will be
    made,
he says, entirely redundant. Swine flu's been and gone but he re-
    fuses
to use any bathroom in our block once quarantined;

the laminated posters taped to their doors at face-height
describe a routine hand-wash lacking in rigour, and he's all too alive
to their dark double meaning – *the power is in your hands* ...

Krishna

You can't punish anyone just
for being beastlike, chomping nectarines with the unembarrassed

air of Keats himself. Why would you want to, anyway?
Because his blue skin irks reality,

because he fucks ten milkmaids at a go
– even if it means being ten men, grown

from the one boy who really scared you – who'd crammed
his young maw with mud

then opened wide to reveal all the planets of heaven
modelled precisely in scaled-down clay, even

the scabbed orb of earth itself, hung
on a yo-yo of spit from the tip of his tongue.

Best Beloved

The dashboard and upholstery got almost too hot to touch those
summer afternoons
we parked the 4x4 outside *Total Tan* to wait for her daughter
barely three years my junior.
Typically with a bucket of chicken from a *KFC* knock-off to share
between us,

piercing each deep-fried breast at our leisure, leaving the knobs of
the wing-bones
rattling against the unctuous cardboard. *Booj's Chicken*, it was,
where we once found in the vat of second-hand toys left behind
for the little ones

a naked Barbie with no head. And when she – no daughter of mine!
– got back to us
her bronze smouldered, hard-won, the sun caught in a rain-cloud.
It made me think
out naked bodies in the first place, unadorned by leaves, must have
been white. I'm not

being racist, it's just my skin never looks quite so naked as yours,
even when
we're framed together on the dance floor, fluttering about like head-
less chickens.
Fine, tans mean wealth now, not manual labour, but there's more.
You want the world

to make you one of its burnished elements, unembarrassable as a
fox in the brush –
like Greek sculpture with the paint worn off, your whiteness risks
becoming only beautiful.
In summer your pale arms and thighs are torchbeams, needless,
almost bone.

I Never Saw a Wild Thing

sorry for itself.
A small bird will drop frozen dead from a bough
without ever having felt sorry for itself.

– D.H Lawrence, 'Self-Pity'

Well, birds obviously enjoy themselves
otherwise a lot of their behaviour makes no sense.
But think that half-second of pure terror
you catch in a wren's eyes

flicking from leaf to leaf –
or those of a goldfish, a gecko, the Kerry Blue terrier,
simplified to a Minuteman,
leaping up from the lino to bite through my jeans;

and even that jheri-curled, thigh-high black thing
was more than a dog, was the pampered child
of the girl who owned it,
whose damaged love kicked and spat like rape.

So forgive us for not going ape,
being descended from those lemmings
who didn't cliff-dive, tree-swinging chimps
less keen to risk the clearing

composted ages hence with not just tree limbs.
Fortune favours the brave only when the brave lucked into fortune
incline to subsidize those
who gesture like them with the chilled salad fork.

Theory

This one goes out to the conspiracy theorists
living off the grid or bunkered in the snow
with his camera-man and his careerist
patter, and asks them gently how they know
the world will end in so many days, but won't
explain to them or to the lens the culture
that shaped such amiable terror as it went
about erecting skyscrapers the actual welder
is brought on screen to tell us didn't fall that way
the nutjobs must believe. If the nutjobs must believe
in a central power somewhere beneath the sky
we must believe in the reporter paid to rove
with a Starbucks coffee in his hand or an iPod™
to convert freaks still tuned in to the voice of God.

Novel

Tendering his plot, sat in his parlour's dark
or knelt on the cold stone of a church to address
a god who won't answer, his overheard face
is lent to the wind and the road he must walk

is gravelly so he must be a smoker or a premature birth;
in his head a voice like a snail secretes its home,
the pillar of his shopping list breaks into blossom –
the wolf man's hands were not covered with fur.

The Wound Speaks

I tell you that which you yourselves do know;
Show you sweet Caesar's wounds, poor dumb mouths,
And bid them speak for me.

– William Shakespeare, *Julius Caesar*

Yes, I'm always getting better. I'm amoral that way.
The blood soaks through the gauze and I am there
at the back of your mind like thinning hair.
I'll take what I can as you know from girl or boy,
blare the muezzin's call of pain until your nerves
are, as they say, shot. I have cut you short
in the middle of what you were saying, darkened your shirt
and not with sweat. I am that in you which loves
to go the extra mile and fly into the building
with your arms full of roses and confront her at her desk.
By dusk I will become the part of you they cannot frisk.
Half-jew, half-nigger, I walk the lightbeam
of a commonplace toward you as you drop the boom.
My eloquence is still allowed. I am the real thing.

TED RICHER

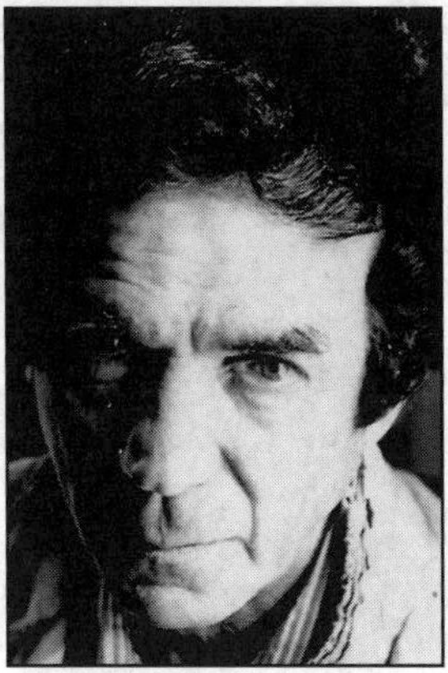

Ted Richer, a graduate of the Iowa Writers' Workshop, teaches at the Massachusetts College of Art and Design in Boston. In 2003 his book, *The Writer in the Story and Other Figurations*, was published in England by the Apocalypse Press. He has published in numerous jourals, including *Agni*, *Literary Imagination,* the T. S. Eliot Society Newsletter, *Harvard Review, James Joyce Quarterly, Leviathan, New York Quarterly,* and *Daedalus*. Richer was the subject of a BBC Radio 3 presentation on *Twenty Minutes*. (Photo courtesy of Magdalena J. Fosse.)

Figuration

In time.

My remains – interred with my bones.

Later.

I waited.

Inscribing – near the grave.

Mourners appeared, and disappeared.

The women, too, circled, veiled.

One witnessed – at a distance.

Withdrawn, she wept.

On guard, the sentinel implored:

"Who's there?"

A figure passed on.

I remained.

Inscribing – near the grave.

Gravediggers clowned:

"In youth when I did love, did love ... "

A skull found, returned.

... poor Yorick!

Still.

A funeral procession drummed along.

Loved ones wailed.

Laureates eulogized.

Ancients cursed.

Immortals, exempt from death, endured.

To be ...

A pilgrim, seeking, journeyed through.

Nearby, a figure of the cross.

Nuns knelt.

The faithful followed.

A priest, in prayer, begged for alms.

Converts, believing, swooned.

Others wandered.

Here.

Mourners reappeared.

The women, too, circled, still veiled.

One witnessed – at a distance.

Withdrawn, she wept.

The sentinel, again, implored:

"Who's there?"

A figure, the same figure, passed on.

I waited, remained.

Inscribing – near the grave.

In time, continued.

The dirge intoned:

– the rest is silence.

So.

Mourners disappeared.

The women, too.

One witnessed – at a distance.

Withdrawn, she wept.

Guarded, the sentinel implored:

"Who's there?"

A figure.

Remains.

Other Times

One time.

She came with me to my room.

We lay on the iron bed.

And.

She said what she said:

"One time – since I like you."

...

Another time.

She came with me to the room.

We lay on the iron bed.

And.

She said what she said:

"This time – since I want you."

...

One other time.

She came with me to the room.

We lay on the iron bed.

And.

She said what she said:

"This time – since I need you."

...

Any other time.

She came with me to my room.

We sat on the iron bed.

And.

She said what she said:

"Any time – when you love me."

Voyeur

Again, she was drawing – in the nude.

Then, she was painting – in the nude.

"Why do you do that?" I said.

"Do what?" she said.

She was swirling her brush on the canvas.

"Paint like that – in the nude?"

She swirled her brush on the canvas.

"My work is my lover –" she sighed.

"My lover is my work."

...

Again, she was drawing – in the nude.

Then, she was painting – in the nude.

"What do you see?" she said.

I stared at what I saw:

"You," I said.

...

Again, she was drawing – in the nude.

Then, she was painting – in the nude.

"What do you see?" she said.

I stared at what I saw:

"Sex," I said.

...

Again, she was drawing – in the nude.

Then, she was painting – in the nude.

"What do you see?" she said.

I stared at what I saw:

"Art," I said.

The Experience

The sight of one in the throes of it.

Or.

The sound of one in the throes of it.

Or.

The scent of one in the throes of it.

Or.

The touch of one in the throes of it.

Or.

The taste of one in the throes of it:

is what I live for ...

And.

The sight of her in the throes of it.

And.

The sound of her in the throes of it.

And.

The scent of her in the throes of it.

And.

The touch of her in the throes of it.

And.

The taste of her in the throes of it:

is what I live for ...

Yet.

The sight of you in the throes of it.

Yet.

The sound of you in the throes of it.

Yet.

The scent of you in the throes of it.

Yet.

The touch of you in the throes of it.

Yet.

The taste of you in the throes of it:

is what I die for ...

Riddance

who

should drag me

out of the house and past the cesspool

across the road   under the fence   through the marsh

into the pond

...

only one

should drag me

out of the house and past the cesspool

across the road   under the fence   through the marsh

into the pond

...

only you

should drag me

out of the house and past the cesspool

across the road   under the fence   through the marsh

into the pond

...

could you

would you

do it now

...

hurry up   please

it's almost time

Swan Song

A dark night.

A long night.

Ice on the ground.

Snow in the air.

Wind.

A lone swan on the pond.

Me – at the window.

...

A darker night.

A longer night.

Ice on the ground.

Snow in the air.

Wind.

A lone swan on the pond.

Me – at the window.

. . .

The darkest night.

The longest night.

Ice on the ground.

Snow in the air.

Wind.

A lone swan on the pond.

Me – at the window.

You gone.

DON SHARE

Don Share is Senior Editor of *Poetry* magazine in Chicago. His books include *Squandermania* (Salt Publishing), *Union* (Zoo Press), and *Seneca in English* (Penguin Classics); forthcoming are *Bunting's Persia* (Flood Editions), and a critical edition of Basil Bunting's poems (Faber and Faber). His translations of Miguel Hernández, collected in *I Have Lots of Heart* (Bloodaxe Books), were awarded the *Times Literary Supplement* Translation Prize, the Premio Valle Inclán, and the PEN/New England Discovery Award. He has been Poetry Editor of *Harvard Review* and *Partisan Review,* Editor of *Literary Imagination,* and Curator of Poetry at Harvard University. (Photo courtesy of Jennifer Flescher.)

Rest

Sabbath is a river that flows
every day but Sunday,
yet there is no rest
from war.

The velocity
of its ferocious light
is its maximum possible velocity,
even in the spired
faculty of the soul
with all her longing and avidity.

Bitter in the belly
but honey in the mouth ~
copious resin of experience ~
are these *cryptonyms, influentials*.

Firmly rooted as dogwoods, as axioms,
each star casts about again
for more of its core to burn

while below,
our sole garden is italicized
by crime, the first and last of things:

Justice is conflict,
not the other way around.

On Being Philosophical

My tendency is to be philosophical before
I even need to be philosophical, which is,
perhaps, the essence of *the thing itself*.

Taking a break from work, for example,
to worry about losing my job,
I ponder why one uses the figure

of a dog thrown a crumb from the table –
what dog relishes a crumb? No, boss,
morsel is the better word (bone, gristle,

chunk, shred, hunk): dogs require
things to devour, being devout gulpers
who by nature leave behind essential drool.

You can't fool a dog with your crumbs.
That's the heart of it, the meat of it.
What you toss they'll jaw up well.

This is muscular, nervy, an act
that contains and embodies its own
completion because dogs do

a great job of waiting, unlike Descartes
or me, needing no mind behind the mind.
Like Descartes, I keep deciding

that foreboding is worth something.
So I eat numberless vegetables to avoid
injury to fellow souls, in spite

of which I am not a virtuous man.
Dogs don't converse while they eat.
We say grace, clink glasses, drink the wine.

Where there's a will, evidently there's ... a *will*.

At Home

Greetings to the red-eyed clouds
from this, the house that sits

on the mound and faces the corner
that marriage built, where wine

was drunk and semen flooded
the egg which lodged in the uterus

that built the daughter who greeted
the man and the woman here

in the mound at the corner in the house
that education built, and you

know from home-schooling
that the woman can be the teacher

and the man can be the tender child
and ditto the actual infant, depending

on her sex, dependent on love and
income; oh our dear dependent

is ruining the new chair in the house
that nested ambition built, along

with naked sense, and the beak
of god, the job of love, the hurt

of older homes, the hang
of it generally, the hands of pain,

the haze of Zoloft and the pudge
of Prozac, the twins of failed

marriages that manage to live on
in the ardor of our redone arbor

here in the house that books built,
that Yiddish and the Book of Common

Prayer built, that Presbyterian pride
built, that pogroms built, that blue

and white collars built, that Bildungs-
romans built, that the Biltmores built,

that mad dogs bayed at, that the baby
was born in that the cat bit and mouse

whispered within, over which, mortgaged,
the thunder caught its tongue and brought

great downpours upon while the coffee boiled,
while the paper, delivered late again, said:

We fight the terrorists abroad
so we don't have to fight them at home.

Sweet Water, Best Bread

Bread, kneaded with rainwater,
failing that, with pure light thin
fountain water that arises in the east
and flows forever eastward, failing
that, water from a quick-running spring
from flinty, chalky, gravelly ground,
failing that, water from the longest river
you can find, failing that, muddy, still,
thick water left to settle for a day or two,
or even well-water lifted in dark old stone
cisterns ~ and if nature won't afford you
these your purest water must then be had
by art at infinite cost, and in rudiments.

Honi Soit ...

– Royal Order of the Garter

"Honi soit qui mal y pense," my father
Mistranslated, and misconstrued, as "Evil
To him who evil does," missing the point. Oh,
I thought about, yet never did evil to my father
Though he cursed and bruised me and saw no evil
In doing so. If he ever laid a hand on a garter,
Would its likely owner, my mother, have wished to appoint
Such bent violence in offering to her own offspring?
Yes, she would, anointing it without even thinking.
So I took his violence unbeaten, as an honor, unblinking.
If my father only knew what was brewing! Each blow
Had rectitude, blessing, intimacy, and a ring
Of the implicative. Yet I did not suppose I was suffering,
Or that he was wicked. Now, a badge of honor, I still don't.

Bookish Men

My mother was apparently quoting Burke
When she would say, *The age of chivalry is gone* ~
Not aptly, though, given her conquering empire
Of barbed irrationality: her marriage
Of inconvenience to Dad, the oafish sons he'd sire,
Not men-at-arms, but men-at-home. . . . berserk
Merciless chivvying, charmless chipping down to bone
In the cheerless shire of shared sham and rage.
The chirography on my birthday cards no relief,
Familiar rites for forty years. Fruitless now to wonder.
A gentleman always carries a handkerchief,
A gentleman never asks a woman her age,
Were not Burke; she sent us into lifelong solitude
Through repetition ... bookish men, old for our years, rude.

A Drop in the Bucket

My mother, not quoting Coleridge: *Water, water*
everywhere, not a single drop to drink.
"Nor" was not her style, nor was her addition
of "single" or dropping of "and" singular.
She added many a word to what my father
failed to say, or said. This was the rule in her
extempore kingdom of sentences and kitchen sink.
She was well-spoken ... unlike my father, dryly brilliant
scientist who seldom said more than he meant ~
nothing token, quotable, or extravagant.
Words, to Dad, were data, nothing to be spoken;
to Mom, syllables strung together, each a token.
My mother wanted to be remembered and quoted;
her magisterium was full-bore, lachrymose, full-throated.

Ontogeny

Recapitulates phylogeny, my mother misquoted.
An admirable *extempore Orator pro Harangue*,
Her world was "hideous undelightful convulsed constricted,"
but in her Penelope's work (*semper* fidelities), weaving
and unweaving maternity, she bent our lumpen tongues
which like boxwood were not easily shaped by the lathe.
There was good and plenty for us to feed on and loathe:
Father's raising crows to peck our eyes out.
Uncle's dying prematurely from a clot.
Our playing at risk of punishment on the spot.
In the end there was too much preoccupation with grieving,
But never mind: among one-eyed fathers mom is blind.
We each began as fingerlings resembling tadpoles, near-fish.
This was our first history. Phylogeny, after all, is selfish.

Looking over My Shoulder

I went to heaven once, sadly
leaving my push-mower and orange snow
shovel behind, like uneaten food
pushed aside on a china plate.

The man upstairs was not happy.
He liked a sharp blade and a clear
driveway. His strictures were

stringent enough to shrive a cactus.
Yet it was I who blindly insisted
on formalities, and stood

on what I thought was ceremony.
I could scarcely taste the beer he poured,
or eat my ham sandwich.

When our visit was over,
he shook my hand and sent me
somersaulting back to my village, where

I was filled, thank God, with genuine salt.

JON STALLWORTHY

Jon Stallworthy's books include *Rounding the Horn: Collected Poems*, prize-winning biographies of Wilfred Owen and Louis MacNeice, *Singing School*, 'the autobiography we would like all poets to write' (*Oxford Today*), critical studies of Yeats's poetry, editions of Owen's *Complete Poems and Fragments* and Henry Reed's *Collected Poems*, translations of the poetry of Alexander Blok and Boris Pasternak, and such anthologies as *The Penguin Book of Love Poetry* and *The Oxford Book of War Poetry*. Having been a Professor of English Literature at Cornell and Oxford, he is now a Senior Research Fellow of Wolfson College, Oxford, and a Fellow of the British Academy. (Photo courtesy of Studio Edmark Photography.)

Pour Commencer

Take 1 green pepper and 2 tomatoes
and cut them into rings and hearts. Mix those
with olives, black olives, and go for a swim
in a green sea with her (or him).
Then serve your salad on two bellies. Pour
a little sun-warmed olive oil in your
salt navel, some vinegar in hers
(or his), and eat slowly with your fingers.
Empty the bottle. Open a second. Then
lick your plates. You will need them again.

The Source

The dead living in their memories
are, I am persuaded, the source
of all that we call instinct.

– W.B. Yeats

Taking me into your body
you take me out of my own,
releasing an energy,
a spirit, not mine alone

but theirs locked in my cells.
One generation after
another, the blood rose and fell
that lifts us together.

Such ancient, undiminished
longings – my longing! Such
tenderness, such famished
desires! My fathers in search

of fulfilment storm through
my body, releasing now
loved women locked in you
and hungering to be found.

The Almond Tree

I

All the way to the hospital
the lights were green as peppermints.
Trees of black iron broke into leaf
ahead of me, as if
I were the lucky prince
in an enchanted wood
summoning summer with my whistle,
banishing winter with a nod.

Swung by the road from bend to bend,
I was aware that blood was running
down through the delta of my wrist
and under arches
of bright bone. Centuries,
continents it had crossed;
from an undisclosed beginning
spiralling to an unmapped end.

II

Crossing (at sixty) Magdalen Bridge
Let it be a son, a son, said
the man in the driving mirror,
Let it be a son. The tower
held up its hand; the college
bells shook their blessing on his head.

III

I parked in an almond's
shadow blossom, for the tree
was waving, waving me
upstairs with a child's hands.

IV

Up
the spinal stair
and at the top
along
a bone-white corridor
the blood tide swung
me swung me to a room
whose walls shuddered
with the shuddering womb.
Under the sheet
wave after wave, wave
after wave beat
on the bone coast, bringing
ashore – whom?
New-
minted, my bright farthing!
Coined by our love, stamped with
our images, how you
enrich us! Both
you make one. Welcome
to your white sheet,
my best poem!

V

At seven-thirty
the visitors' bell
scissored the calm
of the corridors.
The doctor walked with me
to the slicing doors.
His hand upon my arm,
his voice – *I have to tell*
you – set another bell
beating in my head;
your son is a mongol
the doctor said.

VI

How easily the word went in –
clean as a bullet
leaving no mark on the skin,
stopping the heart within it.

This was my first death.
The '*I*' ascending on a slow
last thermal breath
studied the man below

as a pilot treading air might
the buckled shell of his plane –
boot, glove, and helmet
feeling no pain

from the snapped wires' radiant ends.
Looking down from a thousand feet
I held four walls in the lens
of an eye; wall, window, the street

a torrent of windscreens, my own
car under its almond tree,
and the almond waving me down.
I wrestled against gravity,

but light was melting and the gulf
cracked open. Unfamiliar
the body of my late self
I carried to the car.

VII

The hospital – its heavy freight
lashed down ship-shape ward over ward –
steamed into night with some on board
soon to be lost if the desperate
charts were known. Others would come
altered to land or find the land
altered. At their voyage's end
some would be added to, some

diminished. In a numbered cot
my son sailed from me; never to come
ashore into my kingdom
speaking my language. Better not

look that way. The almond tree
was beautiful in labour. Blood-
dark, quickening, bud after bud
split, flower after flower shook free.

On the darkening wind a pale
face floated. Out of reach. Only when
the buds, all the buds, were broken
would the tree be in full sail.

In labour the tree was becoming
itself. I, too, rooted in earth
and ringed by darkness, from the death
of myself saw myself blossoming,

wrenched from the caul of my thirty
years' growing, fathered by my son,
unkindly in a kind season
by love shattered and set free.

Lioness

The Serengeti lioness
arches her back, retracts her claws
to cuff a boisterous cub,
and licks her travelled paws.
She is at home in her body
as you are at home in yours.

The lion that, shamming sleep,
was watching her strolls through
a bevy of princesses
to share her shade. As you
are at home in your body,
I am at home there too.

from *War Poet*

Whenever the child cried out at night,
he would be rescued by a blade of light,
a mother's paper and pencil. 'Draw
me the horror you say you saw,
and your drawing will drive it away.'
Your grown child heard that again today.

I was trying to escape, cutting a path
uphill in the sulphurous aftermath
of some Armageddon, sensed but not seen
in the valley where we had been.
No sound but the bark of a dog, somewhere
ahead or behind us, rasping the air
as we with our gasping, she and I.
Her voice then behind me: 'Look how the sky
Lightens along the ridge. If we can keep
heading for that, who knows, we could sleep
in a happy valley.'
                                        It was true –
the bright ridge a blade to the rescue.
I turned to take her hand, but as I did
her body, like a candle, melted
into smoke, a writhing ghost the wind
Snatched from my arms.
                                        Real or imagined
the animal cry that woke me? Hers
or mine? No exorcist answers
as I write this, and an Arctic light
uncovers the bedspread and the white
pillow warmed, through other nights, by one
whose smile was my sunrise. My un-
returning, subterranean sun.

Before Setting Out

Before setting out on a journey,
the Russians sit down with a glass
of champagne (if they have it) or *kvass*
and take stock of whatever they see
themselves taking or leaving
for others to take or leave,
the luggage of love and grief
'not wanted on voyage'.

An evening,
a garden I think of as mine
(and others have thought of as theirs),
a couple of garden chairs
and, yes, a bottle of wine
to lubricate memory, bring
to this slanting light what has been lost
and found: love first and last,
a splinter of the true sun colouring
the colourless. Eyes return
to spring in a wilderness, once
a garden and a garden since;
a spring in which to learn
the names of apple trees and where
the snowdrop hides that will be found
when children start clearing the ground.
Bonfire smoke sweetens the air.
If only I could learn
from the Russet to let my leaves go
downwind to the bonfire, and so
sweeten the village as others burn
bitterly. We are at war
again, but laughter can be heard
above the axe in the orchard,
wheels slowing at the door.

Constancy

Nothing to do – Constance my love – with you,
at three, nor some would say with me, at three
score years and ten. You will hold other hands,
tell other men you love them (constantly
or not), and some will answer as I do,
and did, a grandfather who understands

almost too late what love might be: desire
not to possess, but share, another's self and world.
Neither in love nor now in sympathy
with my own self and mutilated world,
I sense a simpler love, that would require
only that you be Constance, constantly.

JOHN TALBOT

John Talbot's first book of poems is *The Well-Tempered Tantrum* (2004). His poems have appeared in the *Yale Review, Poetry,* the *American Scholar, Iowa Review, Literary Imagination,* the *Southern Review, Agenda, Poetry Daily, Arion, Southwest Review, Atlanta Review,* and elsewhere on both sides of the Atlantic. They often involve Greek and Latin: his translations from Theocritus appear in the Norton anthology *The Greek Poets* (2009), and his second book of poems, *Rough Translation,* addresses modern versions of Horace and Virgil. His book-length study of ancient lyric metres in English poetry will be published by Duckworth. (Photo courtesy of Brigham Young University.)

JOHN TALBOT

Kindling

You gone, I thought to look
for warmth in the pith of trees,
so I went to the chopping-block,
brought axe's edge to kiss
soft, knotty-hearted pine
whose sinews might warm mine.

Matchstick's rasp, blue chuff:
the fine-shaved kindling caught,
curled into twenty fists
that cupped their fingers shut,
till fire fastened to the wood
and wooed it close and hot,
and soon the room was warm enough
but I was not.

Late Manner

Something expired. At the turning
A spirit was gone. That which was
Turned to sepia: high collars, punting,
Waxed mustaches, parasols.

From bridges, children stared in the river
And felt themselves, also, halved.
Old manners were patently over.
New manners had not yet arrived.

The old, without waiting to speak
Their parting lines in the act,
Learned to exit the way of pipe-smoke.
Uttered nothing. Utter tact.

Steamy ghosts rose from the horses'
Maws as they champed at their bits.
The ladies reached for their purses.
The gentlemen tipped their hats.

After Callimachus

Somebody thoughtless dropped your name:
        "Such a shame
about Heraclitus – and so young."
        I bit my tongue,
but hot tears came. Mind's inward screen
hosted a scrum of flashbacks: long, late-teen
        bull-sessions, bulldozing through
politics, parties, metaphor, rhythm, pun
and punishment, till we'd talked the sun
        out of his sky. But you,

friend, long gone to dust, you're still in touch:
your poems, those living nightingales, still feel
heat of the sun and moonshine. Their songs peal
        forever silvery beyond the all-
        devourer's clutch.

After Horace *Odes* 1.9

So, James, you see that crusty scab atop
The crown of Nobscott Hill? That's all that's left
        Of snowfall that, at Christmastime, we
                Thrilled to, and felt our spirits rising

With every inch it rose. There's something else –
You couldn't feel this way, James, but I did –
        For me the snowflakes fell as hours and
                Minutes; I felt, in each one of them, lapsing

Grains of sand pinched in an hourglass waist.
I'm telling you I feel you slipping. I
        Am slipping, I should say: these quicksand
                Decades (for you that's a lifetime) pull me

Away from you, who pull me by the sleeve
Towards the door that opens on March's thaw,
        And plead for me to throw a baseball
                In a soft arc for your bat to translate

Into a sailing, whistling flash. You're right:
What does it matter where such brightness falls?
        Forget what I've been saying. Somewhere,
                Maybe not far from here, in pigtails,

She catches spring's first sunlight on her cheek,
The girl you'll marry fifteen years from now,
        Pretending not to flirt with boys who,
                Though she's exactly their age, feel younger.

Foreign and Domestic

Caesar has got a war on. He has snatched,
As somebody wrote once, dire peril from
The jaws of safety. Here's how Caesar styled it:
"Mission accomplished."

Well. This calls for celebration. Sandy,
Put up your hair that way you do, and light
The twilight candles, while I telephone for
Takeaway curry,

And if the delivery boy arrives an hour
Late, don't worry, I won't slam the kid.
I've mellowed since the days I used to rage at
Clinton in office.

* * *

Plucked this morning from Nobscott Hill's pitched
Ridges, I transplant you, sapling fir,
Guardian of this new house, roots newly matched
To ours. Be here

Thirty years on, the day I'm slated to sign
Mortgage's last check: when all the grown
Children revisit, and beneath you, pine,
Dandle their own.

* * *

I envy that ancient poet, Horace: fat
(According to his own account) and bald,
But svelt enough to pull off this great coup:
An ode to Venus.

So, can a Christian envy pagans? Yes,
We have a history along those lines. Look, Sandy:
From that cold scarp where brooding has her temple,
        Come down to me.

* * *

Cathedral ceiling vaulting or vaunting above
Flat-screen plasma and hundred-channeled
Console, two-income childless, pre-nup:
        Thin consolation.

Not displeasing: no McMansion in sight,
or bistro called "Avanti." Scatter of children;
me in the kitchen, doing the dishes; you dipping
        Deep in a novel.

– After Horace, Odes *3.14, 3.22, 1.30 and 1.38*

After Horace, *Odes* 4.7

Ice, like the shimmering robe that blond blonde lets drop
To her ankles, slips from the field,
And lets the brook break, chuckling, from its grip.
She can't be twenty years old,

She and her friends, sunbathing girls, who go
Dressed in their daring skin,
Parading everlasting youth – or so
They'd have you think. Think again:

Think of how, six months on, the last sour breath
Of moribund summer's breeze
Will fail, and autumn pummel the grass beneath
Carpets of frost-gilded leaves.

Outside, the seasons mend such damages,
But not so the weather within:
No springtime thaws your limbs, no sun assuages
Once winter gets under your skin.

Onto the very plot on which you'll drop
Your ancestors fell first,
Who yearned for deathless things and tendered hope
And now are shades and dust.

Join them tomorrow? Next month? Who can tell?
Best live today with flair.
The secret accretions of a life led well
Elude the grasping heir.

But learn good judgment now – for all your wit
And pedigree won't budge
When men speak of you in the preterite
And you become the judged.

Stern X, for all his piety, still died.
        Ice will not soon release
Y to her pleading Z. He tried
        To rescue her. She stays.

Nightjar

And if I shrink to drain your flask of pitch?
Call you duskfeather, call you nightjar.
Up and churr then, up and hawk for moths.
Come morning, not crosswise as others do,

But flush along some branch, you'll stretch.
To nut-dun mottle, to bracken strew,
Match your plumage. Reward no twitcher
With soever a twitch. Lapsed creed, you,

You toast of no vintage, you draft
Of afterthought tipped pinging into the butt,
Nightjar. Shallow in those ruts you scored
By the footpath, your paired bald

Eggs will baffle in the sun the toddler
Tomorrow and the toddler's mother.

Property Tax Eclogue

Tityrus, we must leave the sweet fields of home.
– Virgil, *Eclogues* I

Inscribed afternoon. Too like the horse's
Rippling neck, these pale fields billowing
Where the wind ups and rifles. Such discerning
Sifts me. Too much, this soft touch. Get thee
Behind me, satin sunset, knapped in whisper's
Afterburr. False, this smudge of bees that blur
Realtors' terms with pastoral. I am past
Pastoral. Tityrus, we are getting kicked
Flat on our taxes. We are getting shown
The low road out of Sudbury, thank you three
Car garage and vaulted great room new
Construction in executive neighborhood
Neighborless horse property. The rich
Plot hurts where I have stooped to its rough kiss.

Windfall

1

Bright brittle grief abseiling back through plummet
Space onto pursed roots. Leaves paying out
And paying back. How right to stand shin deep

Among our cast-offs, and to tread fat summer's
Surfeit, more real as crunching underfoot
Than when, as pale incipient buds, they seemed

To sing their green inhaling. But for riches
Nothing can touch our long slow holding out.
Its music I know is *sotto*, and only reaches
Age's inner hearing. The year is out,

Dog-eared our books, our federal windfall spent,
Papery cadences of a season tuned
To turnover, the broken and the rent
Slow music of the sap in its slow wound.

2

Are you an answer then, blood-russet shards,
October parchment, spiraling towards the pile
Where grooved roots buckle? My question is not hard:
What are we bound for? Your afflicted style

Glosses the chapped lawn's needling. You have earned
Undoing, so composingly you drop,
Burning to be given to be burned
By those who loved you. This is over-ripe,

I am over ripeness, I require some binding.
Make me an omnium-gatherum whose pages
Recall the trees that gave both bud and rending,

Those stooping veterans stripping off their badges.
It is good for everything to be ending
Again. My hope is reddening at the edges.

HARRY THOMAS

Harry Thomas was born in Alaska, on Gutenberg's birthday, but grew up in southern California. Educated there and at the University of Michigan, he studied with Robert Hayden, Radcliffe Squires, and Joseph Brodsky. For Penguin UK he edited the *Selected Poems of Thomas Hardy* and *Montale in English*. In 2001 he founded a literary imprint, Handsel Books, for Other Press, an affiliate of Random House. Handsel's list includes books by Leslie Epstein, Lee Gerlach, Peter Jungk, and Stanley Plumly. After living in Boston for 25 years, he and his wife, the potter Adriana Pazmany, have returned to California. Poems here first appeared in *Slate, Literary Imagination, The Southern Review,* and *The Formalist*. (Photo courtesy of Harry Thomas.)

Of Country I Know

for David Ferry

Above the lower tree line in the desert
northeast of San Diego, where I'm from,
in land mapped out abruptly by the sun,
you'll find a spreading growth of pinion pine,
juniper, branching nearly to the ground,
lilac and sage, and scattering white pines.
Even in the driest months of summer
(in some years summer lasts through late November)
where there are seeds and insects there will be birds
and small, ground-dwelling, furtive creatures too.
Hummingbirds nest in the cactus scrub;
woodpeckers bore homes in the crazy yuccas;
meadowlarks shelter in the slender reeds;
lizards slip in and out of rock crevices,
panting and scurrying on the hot sands;
coyotes prowl all night for a square meal.

Everywhere life goes on against the odds.
You stand in the middle of a riverbed
that wind has driven down since there was wind
and like as not, three feet below the surface,
rimmed with a crust of alkaline deposits,
or where there's mesquite or a clump of bunch grass,
there's water left from last year's winter rains.

Mt Palomar

for my brother Charlie

The tour had lasted nearly an hour already,
and what with the slow walk in the heat to the dome,
and the docents' recitations and dumb jokes,
the children in tow appeared eager to go home,

though in the dome's dim light it was hard to tell,
and much of the time, I confess, I was all ears
to learn that mother's Corning made the great mirror –
made two, in fact, the first one a failure; that years

went by, George Ellery Hale growing frailer,
before the polishers in Cal Tech's shop
were finally done – the War deflecting them,
the Pyrex/silica disk covered up;

that the huge horseshoe tube that holds the mirror,
a million-pound precision instrument,
floats on a mere 3/1000ths of an inch of oil,
the pressure of one hand enough to move it;

that the dome, bigger than the Pantheon,
rotates on tracks so smoothly no vibration's
transmitted to the telescope; that when
the telescope at last looked at the heavens

the photographs of spiral nebulae
proved once again the universe's expansion,
a theory even Einstein had disputed
until, in '31, he visited Mt. Wilson.

Then we were taken through an opened door
and told to stand along the metal catwalk
that runs around the dome, the sunlight blinding.
And as a docent started in to yak –

"That small dome there's the Oscar Meyer dome" –
I felt a movement under me. "Hold on,"
I said. And everyone looked wonderstruck,
and braced themselves for orbiting the sun.

Seasonal

for Adriana

Three months of winter. Absence
is all here. Absence of sun-
light on the icy streams and
in the hickory branches
lined with snow. Absence of leaves:
the trees reduced to rigid
quadrants, geometric graphs.

A brutal, aimless absence,
where at evening I have seen
pairs of robins foraging
for the fermented sweetness
of wrinkled apples. They peck
and pivot above the fields
like sparks on the wintry air.
Yet, more than once, a sick male
has mistaken a window,
wavering with warmth, for an
open, unending passage,
angled against it, and died.

Three months of winter. Absence
of love, not less than sunlight,
fails me. And then this evening
a hint at return: a plane,
seemingly a moth, winged by
and, reflected in the cold
glass on the desk where I read,
silently entered my ear,
as though it would propel me
to some presence, maybe yours.

The House of the Customs Men

You don't remember the house of the customs men
on the hillside above the cliff overhanging the reef.
Desolate, it has waited for you since the evening when
the swarm of your thoughts entered it
and stopped, irresolute.

Southwest winds have lashed the old walls for years
and the sound of your laughter has lost its gaiety.
The compass or no reason at all goes crazy,
and the dice come up numbers no one guesses.
You don't remember; another time confuses
your memory, a thread's being lost.

I hold an end of it still; but the house
draws away and the smoke-blackened weathercock
on the rooftop whirls unpitying.
I'm holding an end; but you stay alone,
not breathing here in the dark.

Oh the fleeting horizon! where the light
of a tanker rarely flashes.
Is there a way through here? (The sea still crashes
against the crumbling cliff.)
You don't remember the house of this evening of mine.
And I don't know who goes and who remains.

– from the Italian of Eugenio Montale

Grandfather

You weighed so little when I picked you up
from off the kitchen floor where you had died
that morning making coffee, the white cup
now shattered into pieces at your side,
and you – exposed through your white boxer's fly,
and took you to the back room to your bed
and laid you down and sat and waited. I –
I was sixteen. My first time with the dead.

I sat there on the bed as if to stay,
not going out to grandma and my brother
despite their desperate crying out for you.
I watched the palm fronds in the window sway
in the warm summer air…And then my mother,
then paramedics, came, and I withdrew.

Elegy

Having driven two hundred miles through towns
of strangers, by cabins, trailers, Mormon outposts,
I have come, brother, to your mountain grave,
a month too late to do my part in the service,
and years too late to set things right between us.
What words are there after so long a silence –
the need to make a living took me from you,
and then the life you chose took you from me?
Let a few wildflowers and an old love be all,
brother, you have from me forever. Farewell.

– *after Catullus*

The Little Girl of Pompeii

Because everyone's anguish is our anguish, we
Go on reliving yours, thin little girl

Who held yourself convulsively to your mother
As though you wanted to be inside her again

When in the afternoon the sky turned black.
No use, because the air becoming poison

Filtered to find you through the closed windows
Of your peaceful, solidly built house, already

Made happy by your singing and shy smile.
Centuries have passed, the ash has petrified,

Imprisoning forever your soft limbs.
So you will remain among us, contorted chalk,

Endless agony, terrible testimony
To how little the gods care for our poor seed.

But nothing remains of your faraway sister,
The young Dutch girl walled up within four walls,

Who nevertheless wrote of her futureless youth.
Her mute dust has been scattered by the wind,

Her brief life locked inside a worn-out notebook.
Nothing remains of the Hiroshima schoolgirl,

A wall shadow cast by the light of a thousand suns,
A victim sacrificed on the altar of fear.

You, powerful ones, owners of new poisons,
Sad secret keepers of the definitive thunder,

The sky's afflictions are more than enough for us.
Before you push the button, stop and consider.

November 20, 1978

– from the Italian of Primo Levi

Deor

Wayland in Varmland
suffered adversities,
that strong-minded man
knew misery.
Bitter setbacks, pains
of winter colds, these
were his companions.
His truck was with trouble
after Nithhad had done
the violence to him –
hacking his hamstrings,
hobbling the better man.
    – That was endured,
    so may this be.

Beadohilde despaired
when her brothers were butchered,
but when she was sure
she carried a child –
that was what wrecked her.
She couldn't conceive
of a future.
    – That was endured,
    so may this be.

We've all of us heard
how the Geat loved Mathilde,
loved her without limit,
loved with such love
his sleep was shattered.
    – That was endured,
    so may this be.

Thirty years Theoderic
ruled the Maeringa's town.
The facts are all known.
    – That was endured,
    so may this be.

We all know of Eormanric
and his wolflike ways –
subjugating subjects
the length of Gottland.
He was a cruel king!
Men sat unmoving,
shackled to sorrow.
thinking just one thing –
to cut the king down.
    – That was endured,
    so may this be.

Of myself I'll say this:
I was once the poet
of the Heodingas,
dear to my lord.
My name was Deor.
Winter to winter
I had a good holding,
a lavishing lord.
Now one Heorrenda,
a masterly man,
finds praise in the place
until lately my lord
gave to me.
    – That was endured,
    so may this be.

– from the Anglo-Saxon, c. 725

ROSANNA WARREN

Rosanna Warren teaches English and Comparative Literature at Boston University. Her book of criticism, *Fables of the Self: Studies in Lyric Poetry*, came out in 2008. Her next book of poems, *Ghost in a Red Hat,* is forthcoming in March 2011. Other titles include *Stained Glass, Each Leaf Shines Separate, Snow Day,* and *Departure*. With Stephen Scully, she translated *Suppliant Women* by Euripides (1995). In 1989, she edited *The Art of Translation: Voices from the Field*. She is a fellow of the American Academy of Arts and Sciences, and Secretary of the American Academy of Arts and Letters. Poems here first appeared in *American Scholar, Berlin Journal, Fulcrum,* the *New York Review of Books,* the *New Yorker, Northwest Review, Poetry,* and *Slate*. (Photo courtesy of Charlie Mars-Mahlau.)

ROSANNA WARREN

[illegible]

Intermezzo, Piano Solo

Those teasing notes, descending, reverse themselves,
the whole piece mirrors itself upside and down.
Your fingers find their way, moving by heart
(sotto voce) from one thicket to another,
registering (dolente) in the soft tissue of fingerprints
what a poverty of notes, how richly strung –
as your kisses (perdendosi) repeat themselves
from one hour, one day, to the next, but never the same.
And now that you're gone (diminuendo), the andante strays
imperfectly in my mind. The nights are long,
meridional, raucous. I see now, purity
was just an effect of inexperience.
In the street below, the kids (crescendo) curse till dawn,
practice fellatio by streetlight, pressed to the wall.

Aubade

Silver gelatin the fine outline of the window sash at dawn
but morning turned blind eyes to us nor could
I see you   Sleep had cobwebbed you like a pharaoh
and later when we walked in the frozen field we cracked every
    mirror
Swamp grasses ticked against each other
Metallic puddles showed us nothing not even our shadows
My shadow asked your shadow where was the lost child
Mahler said for a soft sound don't give it to the oboe but
only to some monster instrument that must struggle and force
beyond its natural range to murmur or hum
We outpaced our shadows   We were looking for the place
where light would cry out when ice sliced its hands
but we found instead the crimson reishi fungus ruffled in its
    petticoat
Ganoderma lucidum from which a healing tea could be boiled
though we abstained left it on its stump and returned with our
    palms empty
hungry for night eager
for another dawn

Liszt, Overheard

Jet-lagged, half-insomniac, I lie in a dim tower
in a foreign college as piano notes ripple up
the winding stair. It's medieval here,
spliced Renaissance spliced late Victorian.
I'm an emigrant from my life. Now a violin
teases the piano, a cello breathes heavily on both –
an audience must be straining forward in a panelled hall.
How many years have I half-heard
a music meant for others? The chestnut trees
shrug epaulets and fringes in the night wind.
Black tulips sway. An arpeggio falls downstairs.
Your face surges, known and strange, its history drawn
by an Old Master who worked only in the dark.

Aftermath

Dawn. The moment it was
it was over.

– Deborah Tall

It was that last, euphoric summer, between
one chemo and another, when you looked out
your kitchen window and saw the doe standing
at the edge of your lawn where the thicket gathers –
autumn olive, buckthorn, forsythia, dogwood.
And when you stepped outside, the doe stayed still
and looked in your eyes, you thought, with a companionable
complicit question, and didn't run. You were
light-headed. The doe lowered her nose
to shove at the small bundle at her feet
folded up like an awkward deck chair
till then invisible in its hollow of grass.
She had just given birth. The fawn couldn't stand
but raised its too-large head to gaze at you.
You were, as you said, already more or less
posthumous. You took each other in.
One of you before, the other beyond fear.
Two creatures, side effects on one another,
headed in opposite directions.

A Kosmos

You lay in your last sleep, not-sleep,
head tilted stiffly to the right on the pillow
at a sharper angle than when you bent over poems,
year after year, and we plucked at each other's lines,

as if now you considered some even starker question.
Your I.V. tubes were gone. Your arms were bruised.
A blue cloth cap enfolded your pale, bald head.
It was too late to give you the lavender shawl I'd imagined

more for my sake than for yours.
Your mouth was suddenly tender, the mouth of a girl.
You had come very far, to come here.
Never one not look at things squarely,

now you looked inward. Who knows what you saw.
And when, weeks later, we gathered
again at the house to say those formal farewells,
I went up to your study looking for *Leaves of Grass*

and found, instead, your orderly desk, unused,
your manuscripts neatly stacked, the framed
photographs of your girls, and, like a private message
from Whitman, who saw things whole, the small

dried body of a mouse. A kosmos, he too. He too, luckier.

Man in Stream

You stand in the brook, mud smearing
your forearms, a bloodied mosquito on your brow,
your yellow T-shirt dampened to your chest
as the current flees between your legs,
amber, verdigris, unraveling
today's story, last night's travail ...

You stare at the father beaver, eye to eye,
but he out-stares you – you who trespass in his world,
who have, however unwilling, yanked out his fort,
stick by tooth-gnarled, mud-clabbered stick,
though you whistle vespers to the wood thrush
and trace flame-flicker in the grain of yellow birch.

Death outpaces us. Upended roots
of fallen trees still cling to moss-furred granite.
Lichen smolders on wood-rot, fungus trails in wisps.
I wanted a day with cracks, to let the godlight in.
The forest is always a nocturne, but it gleams,
the birch tree tosses its change from palm to palm,

and we who unmake are ourselves unmade
if we know, if only we know
how to give ourselves in this untendered light.

Porta Portese

– if it once gleamed, if it ticked, if it buzzed, if it
        oiled eternal youth, if it whispered
on an old tape with the sexual lure of infinite
        cash, if it said I am your private
castle and you are a queen, if it lit a thousand
        bulbs, if it shaved a thousand hairs, if
it declared God loves you, if it promised
        to cure harelips excema scabies rage,
if it clipped hangnails, if it delivered proverbs, if it hugged
        the ass – it's laid out on a collapsible
table or a mat on asphalt, money will change
        hands, money will change us
all, change Gypsies professors Nigerian whores
        limping children drugged babies
i-Podded teens Somali refugees artists in
        drag illegal Albanians cruising pols We said
one world We said isn't my money good enough
        for you Switch blade Switch banks The Cloaca
Maxima accepts all currencies The Tiber
        leaks yellow between its legs venereal
venerable duty-free luxurious silken rippling
        classical waves sold and soldered solved reflected here –

Fire

It would take a voodoo skull, one eye darkened,
one candle-lit, to see

into these pictures. Who set that fire? Who piled
that cliff of smoke? The newsprint

is jaundiced, ripped at the edge.
I set that fire, I piled

that bombastic, mountaining smoke.
I mound it up every night and I don't haul anyone out.

The bodies are stiff, like little T-squares.
It's not clear what geometry problem they solve.

The ditch is a rampart.
The live ones, turbaned, stand on the upper rim.

Bombed trucks burn rectangularly.
The books on Mutanabi Street make a chunky oatmeal mush.

This world, the same for all, was shaped by no god or man
but always was and will be

an everlasting fire, said Heraclitus. And the child
in the charred room reaches out to touch the wall:

the furniture's burned, his father's shot, the mirror
reflects only the camera flash.

We found fire in our souls before
we stole it from heaven.

Now we are the lords of light
and the darkroom is ours.

Mediterranean

– when she disappeared on the path ahead of me
I leaned against a twisted oak, all I saw was evening light where
 she had been:

gold dust light, where a moment before
and thirty-eight years before that

my substantial mother strode before me in straw hat, bathing suit,
 and loose flapping shirt,
every summer afternoon, her knapsack light across her back,

her step, in sandals, firm on the stony path
as we returned from the beach

and I mulled small rebellions and observed the dwarfish cork
 trees
with their pocky bark, the wind-wrestled oaks with arms akimbo,

while shafts of sea-light stabbed down between the trunks.
There was something I wanted to say, at the age of twelve,

some question she hadn't answered,
and yesterday, so clearly seeing her pace before me

it rose again to the tip of my tongue, and the mystery was
not that she walked there, ten years after her death,

but that she vanished, and let twilight take her place –

Ocular

So damp the pages of novels curl up like vine leaves,
the stories smear. In the Métro this morning
a man was scraping a poster from the wall:

all the promised felicity hung in shreds.
My eye is swollen, purple. I can't read, near
or far. My childhood is far.

I slept on a naked mattress the pit bull ripped;
it reeked of smoke, needles littered the floor.
I starved myself, I admired my delicate ribs,

the leaves of a petrified prehistoric fern.
I was prehistoric, my eye teeth turned to fangs.
Day marched in carrying night on his shoulders,

a wizened old man. I preferred night.
Come to me, I said, I'll kiss you anyway,
even if you're ancient and I'm blind and bruised,

we'll laugh, we'll be the Book of Revelation,
I'll wear lingerie from the crypt and we'll eat at the Loveless Café
where biscuits steam and no one spits in the jam.

That was years ago. Night's tired now,
we've worn each other out. We hardly meet.
But I still have one good eye, and when I squint,

you wouldn't believe what I see.

RACHEL WETZSTEON

Rachel Wetzsteon was born in 1967, and was the author of three collections of poems, *The Other Stars* (Penguin, 1994), *Home and Away* (Penguin, 1998), and *Sakura Park* (Persea, 2006), as well as a critical study of W. H. Auden. A fourth collection, *Silver Roses,* will be published by Persea in 2010. Her work has received awards from the National Poetry Series, the Ingram Merrill Foundation, and the American Academy of Arts and Letters. Until her death in 2009, she was Associate Professor of English at William Paterson University, served as poetry editor for the *New Republic,* and resided in Manhattan. (Photo courtesy of Star Black.)

Sunrise over Low

This view is new: gray dome set in a pink sky
like a gem in a ring, rooftops confirming

levels attained, and plump watertowers
perching on each one, my trusty protectors.

It seemed I would not flee old haunts so much
as rise above them, snug in penthouse wisdom.

But daybreak springs its surprises like a shy face
after a drink too many: the dome rebukes me

for spines not cracked, and the banners of dawn
are teases, are sorrows, are prizes, are hunters.

(Once I took a vacation from my vocation.
Getting out of bed was never so easy

yet the sunrise suffered so: where were the clouds
like camels, the fresh day's difficult red riddles?)

The morning rouses itself into gorgeous disquiet.
And as I head out to meet it, run wild,

you Birnam wood of watertowers, you raw sky
trying on colors like a girl before a dance.

Love and Work

In an uncurtained room across the way
a woman in a tight dress paints her lips
a deeper red, and sizes up her hips
for signs of ounces gained since yesterday.

She has a thoughtful and a clever face,
but she is also smart enough to know
the truth: however large the brain may grow,
the lashes and the earrings must keep pace.

Although I've spread my books in front of me
with a majestic air of *I'll show her*,
I'm much less confident than I'd prefer,
and now I've started pacing nervously.

I'm poring over theorems, tomes and tracts.
I'm getting ready for a heavy date
by staying up ridiculously late.
But a small voice advises, Face the facts:

go on this way and you'll soon come to harm.
The world's most famous scholars wander down
the most appalling alleyways in town,
a blond and busty airhead on each arm.

There is an inner motor known as lust
that makes a man of learning walk a mile
to gratify his raging senses, while
the woman he can talk to gathers dust.

A chilling vision of the years ahead
invades my thoughts, and widens like a stain:
a barren dance card and a teeming brain,
a crowded bookcase and an empty bed...

What if I compromised? I'd stay up late
to hone my elocutionary skills,
and at the crack of dawn I'd swallow pills
to calm my temper and control my weight,

but I just can't. Romantics, so far gone
they think their lovers live for wisdom, woo
by growing wiser; when I think of you
I find the nearest lamp and turn it on.

Great gods of longing, watch me as I work
and if I sprout a martyr's smarmy grin
please find some violent way to do me in;
I'm burning all these candles not to shirk

a night of passion, but to give that night
a richly textured backdrop when it comes.
The girl who gets up from her desk and dumbs
her discourse down has never seen the flight

of wide-eyed starlings from their shabby cage;
the fool whose love is truest is the one
who knows a lover's work is never done.
I'll call you when I've finished one more page.

Pemberley

The park was very large. We drove
for some time through a beautiful wood
until the wood ceased, and the house came into view.
Inside were miniatures, small faces
we gawked at until a housekeeper showed us
the master's finer portrait in an upper room.
I dredged up a shaming moment:
you asked me a question, then ducked as I spewed
an idiot's vitriol, blindness disguised as rage.
The house stood well on rising ground,
and beneath its slopes the thirsty couples
held their glasses high at Café Can't Wait.
I spent time at its flimsy tables
but then I walked under trees whose leaves
exhaled gusty stories of good deeds;
I learned empty houses are excellent teachers;
I sent you away and felt you grow
tremendous in your absence. Ask me again.

Short Ode to Screwball Women

On sullen nights like these
when my spirit counts its woes like pearls on a string,
you bring me armfuls of spare pantsuits
and clear-eyed hints about the woman
who might kick up her heels in them, flooding rooms
with cunning, air, an almost gaudy vitality.

Gaudy but sober: when your wayward husband
courted the heiress, you stormed her gates
disguised as a floozy – and asked the butler
to serve you gingerale. It was life
you'd rather be drunk on, roaring life
that told you there is no time for spirits
of dark staircases, only lightning ruses
that not only leave no bruises but give
all parties their wish: rinsed vision and second chances.

Losing a boot heel and giddily claiming
I was born on the side of a hill is easy.
For every such moment there are ten
when my ideal snags midflight, a bag caught in branches.
But a girl can dream, can realize, high
on heroines, that she is mortal
and therefore fearless; that sanity
supplies the ground bass to the wildest singing;
that breezes made visible make the finest winds.

At the Zen Mountain Monastery

A double line of meditators sits
on mats, each one a human triangle.
Evacuate your mind of clutter now.
I do my best, squeezing the static and
the agony into a straight flat line,
but soon it soars and dips until my mind's
activity looks (you can take the girl ...)
uncannily like the Manhattan skyline.
Observe your thoughts, then gently let them go.
I'm watching them all right, unruly dots
I not only can't part from but can't help
transforming into restless bodies – they're
no sooner being thought than sprouting limbs,
no longer motionless but striding proudly,
beautiful mental jukeboxes that play
their litanies of joy and woe each day
beneath the shadow of enormous buildings.
Desires are your jailers; set them free
and roam the hills, smiling archaically.
It's not a pretty picture, me amid
high alpine regions in my urban black,
huffing and puffing in the mountain air
and saying to myself, I'm trying but
it's hopeless; though the tortures of the damned
make waking difficult, they are my tortures;
I want them raucous and I want them near,
like howling pets I nonetheless adore
and holler adamant instructions to –
sprint, mad ambition! scavenge, hopeless love
that begs requital! – on our evening stroll
down Broadway and up West End Avenue.

Largo

"Look for someone to make you slow."
– Elias Canetti

They are ogling the stars in an outdoor garden,
and the night's infectious energy
makes them bold, makes him grab her hands and declare
A brilliant chapter begins tonight:
I have novels in me, whole realms of feeling
your eyes prise open. To which she responds
I'm a changeling, darling, in your masterful hands;
this morning I was one of eight million stories
but now I'm wearing freshwater pearls
at the end of a pier, in the middle of summer –
race me there, and the waves will envy our speed.

A sudden hush descends over Café Largo
and a low voice whispers, Be all these things,
ring all these changes on each other
but slowly. The brain that races tonight
will end up a frowning skull in a viewless mansion;
you'll wake up in bare rooms, horrible jewels in your hands.
Walk, instead, past never-finished cathedrals;
light one cigarette from another;
find, if you know what's good for you, endless answers to whether
the table is really there when you close your eyes.

from *Thirty-Three*

[IX]

When you've drunk too much, time garbles just like speech.
I'm sipping here, sitting my scotch and thinking

of the stories I'll tell with thirty-three more years behind me:
how I finally quit my band, the Repercussions

and formed a new one, the Gem-like Flames
whose soulful lyrics even critics loved.

How I sold the house where I grew up,
dark palace of cloakroom wit and armchair courage,

and only stayed in places which obeyed
the following rules: lawn as large as garden,

zero carpets, bookcases with lived-in look.
How noted film star, Teri Dactyl, wanted to buy

the rights to the saga of my life
and how I refused – I wasn't done with it yet.

By now I'm wording my slurs and getting sleepy,
but thirty-three years on, ah the stories I'll tell.

[X]

In another story it would end like this:
when the heart grew weak from too many lashings,

when the soulmates vanished or disappointed,
she took off for a penthouse greenhouse

where lilies danced in a fan's warm breezes
and nothing could touch her. And sure enough

nothing did: not her unborn blushes,
let alone guests from the cold, with their glad red faces.

Her greenhouse turned green with clippings. But then
one night, sipping strong mint tea, she remembered

the stir a branch makes when spring rain bends it,
how it dips and veers in joy, in fear, for dear life.

The splendor of all her wounds waiting to happen
entered her, and she wrote a story:

"I summon hunger and risk, those lovely
scattershot graces," was the way it began.

Sakura Park

The park admits the wind,
the petals lift and scatter

like versions of myself I was on the verge
of becoming; and ten years on

and ten blocks down I still can't tell
whether this dispersal resembles

a fist unclenching or waving goodbye.
But the petals scatter faster,

seeking the rose, the cigarette vendor,
and at least I've got by pumping heart

some rules of conduct: refuse to choose
between turning pages and turning heads

though the stubborn dine alone. Get over
"getting over": dark clouds don't fade

but drift with ever deeper colors.
Give up on rooted happiness

(the stolid trees on fire!) and sweet reprieve
(a poor park but my own) will follow.

There is still a chance the empty gazebo
will draw crowds from the greater world.

And meanwhile, meanwhile's far from nothing:
the humming moment, the rustle of cherry trees.

KIERON WINN

Kieron Winn was educated at Tonbridge School and at Christ Church, Oxford, where he was awarded a doctorate for his thesis on Herbert Read and T.S. Eliot. His poems have appeared in many magazines, including *Agenda, Agni,* the *Dark Horse,* the *London Magazine, Oxford Magazine, Oxford Poetry, Plectrum, Poetry Review, The Rialto, The Spectator,* the *Swansea Review,* and the *Times Literary Supplement,* as well as in a short film about his work on BBC1. A selection of his poems appears in the anthology *Oxford Poets 2007* (Carcanet). He was awarded the University of Oxford's English Poem on a Sacred Subject Prize in 2007. He lives in Oxford, where he is a freelance teacher. (Photo courtesy of Eleanor Sepanski.)

The Gentleman Bowls Along

for Peter Conrad

The gentleman bowls along, and flourishing his cane
Creates new symbols in the morning air.
His face is sanguine-pink, his waistcoat half unbuttoned;
His liquid eyes reflect stout cattle, orderly hedge;
His brimming heart spills some runaway laughter.
With happiness to hand in breathing, seeing,
Paradise for man cannot be far away.

From the Steamer Back Across Ullswater

Chunks and flails of icy Viking water,
Waves like shrouds, disinterested schelly:
Cold as the ancient rocks above the valley
Whose fearless faces give no hope of quarter.

But I have been tough and snug on the sloping heath,
Where sights through breaks in mist redraw my borders,
In familiar pelts, the way as long or short as
I choose, my freedom in the steaming breath.

Wordsworth and Coleridge

Insufficient, the broad
Oaten flakes,
The convictions plain
As Skiddaw –

How Coleridge would have loved
Neon, glutamates
And so many channels:
Intricate, hare-like, in the end a nuisance.

Unforgetting

Flat shining fields of sand, the shallow-carving
Tigris and Euphrates of the beach streams
Where individual flying grains are seen,
The wet compactions out of which grew keeps
I used to raze with greyish slapped moat water,
Enthralled and never doubting I was loved,
Blue-black rock, its surface softened by salt,
Like miniature coast the coming wave would ruin,
Caves that had ground no man had trodden – all
Stored when the soul passed here before this life,
Restarted by a sleepy train's long snaking.

A Victorian Dreams of Heaven

Let Heaven be a great sweet thaw
Of love gone cold in time or the grave;
The taking of hands
Never thought to be taken again;
The old light in the eyes;

Let Heaven be a great sweet thaw
Of love made numb by jealousy,
Love that dared not act because
Acting would scald and scar like fire.
Let Heaven be an utter release from fear.

Victorians

Near our Victorian house, Victorian graves.
That age's loss of God can still be seen:
A realism in the grains of the day,
As though the Heavenly glory has expired,
Leaving the railway and the angular cranes,
The straggling blackberries and the merchant Thames.

Slowly, I trawl an open hand along
A cold wet street sign, and the living carbon
Meets iron with a kind of holy aptness,
Far from ideas and far from centuries.

July

Ice creams, veranda, sparkling Cornish bay:
Old men look jaunty-classic in the sunlight,
Roman consuls slightly down at heel,
And children swim out to a diving platform
Beyond the boats with names of girls and fays.
On the unwinding vein-like roads, all trammels
Are running out before the sea; in fields
The chlorophyll in salty grass is yielding
Willingly to candescent lifting light.
Elsewhere, the verdant Agincourt discipline
Of men-of-Kent trees, cut out from the pattern,
Long hourless afternoons in pubs on greens;
And on the fellsides, nature at her gaudy,
Old catholic colours in the sky and thorn,
Lake like a giant blue tough-skinned basking lizard,
All colours thick as in a childhood film stock.
In Oxford, students sleek with many an A
Dawdle down the river, playing their part,
And languid fellows decorate the meadows;
Imperial ironies are cultivated
In their straw hats and floppy creasing suits.
Summer professional yet legendary:
Great banner in the heavens, read by all.

Waking

Beside you in the landscape of the bed,
A lightsome cellular warmth behind the eyes,
Balance and hunger, coolness on the covers,
Each muscle moved a full rewarding joy,
Half-dreaming of tea with the distant and the dead,
Your flesh the colour of rose and half-shadows,
Your warmth annihilating metaphysics,
A great ring of light through a flaw in the window,
And then the radio alarm clock coughs
And brings our armour with the needless first word: gunmen.

St Ives

Ash and dust were blown from me by those
Vast and simple packs and bands of colour:
Nutritious, licorous, mackerel-tinted waves,
A solid lapis sky, and platinum sand
That made a massy drawstring purse in the palm.
Dashing and surfing rays were missing nothing,
Lighting every door and stone and corner
To plain and storybook equality,
And mildness I remember as a child,
A nobody, before such adult forces.

Ambleside to Glenridding

for Amanda Holton

The eighteenth century notes Rydal Water
Glittering in a prospect. By Scandale Beck
Climb on a pony track past meteorite-grottoes
To High Sweden Bridge, a lone constructed eye,
A glimpse of civilization, then press on
To a prehuman valley in the mountains
Networked by veins of thin and plashable streams.
Now up, an easy up, with Fairfield left,
Mist and moisture cool on grateful limb,
Loved wideness, thereness, love like sun on stone,
To a broken ridge, the start of dirty walking,
Oikish grass and ankle-killing holes,
But there is light and we have time and food;
So Brothers Water inches round a hill,
Lake like a flat grey pebble, and reaching earth
We head past waterfall and fiery fern,
Past Goldrill to the silver spill of Ullswater,
Its miles of absolute edge as mild as Jesus,
Then to the Travellers Rest for woods-floor beer,
Rich seasoned beef, potatoes piping, whisky
And shortbread, fire and sugar for the next day.

CODA

GEOFFREY HILL

Geoffrey Hill was born in 1932. He has taught at the University of Leeds, the University of Cambridge, and Boston University. He has published a dozen books of poetry, of which the most recent is *A Treatise of Civil Power* (Penguin, 2007), as well as his *Collected Critical Writings* (edited by Kenneth Haynes, Oxford University Press, 2008). At Oxford he read English (Keble College). His poems constituted the Fantasy Poets pamphlet Number Eleven (1952), and he edited *Oxford Poetry* (with Donald Hall, 1953). His *Collected Poems* appeared in 1985 (Penguin), and his *Selected Poems* in 2006 (Penguin; Yale, 2009). In June 2010 he was both elected the Professor of Poetry at Oxford and awarded an Hon. D.Litt. from the University of Oxford. The three uncollected poems reprinted here are from the Fantasy Poets pamphlet Number Eleven (1952), *The Isis,* 19 November 1952, and (with corrections) *Paris Review* 8 (1955), and are courtesy of Geoffrey Hill.

For Isaac Rosenberg

Princes dying with damp curls
In the accomplishment of fame
Keep, within the minds of girls,
A bright imperishable name –
And no one breaks upon their game.

Yet men who mourn their hero's fall,
Laying him in tradition's bed –
With high-voiced chantings and the tall
Complacent candles at his head –
Still leave much carefully unsaid.

When probing Hamlet was aware
That Death in a worn body lay
Cramped beneath the lobby-stair –
(Whose mystery was burnt away
Through the intensity of decay) –

It followed, with ironic sense,
That he himself, who ever saw
Beneath the skin of all pretence,
Should have been carried from the floor
With shocked, tip-toeing drums before.

With ceremony thin as this
We tidy death; make life as neat
As an unquiet chrysalis
That is a symbol of defeat:
A worm in its own winding-sheet ...

Summer Night

The air yields to the nudging owl
Stressing the dark with its long call
Over the coppice and the pool:
Silence has stirred inside this shell.

The dark creaks like an empty house:
(There is nothing, over the white fields, amiss)
Though like the air the untroubled water flows,
Time stands upon its toes.

Overhead move the tense stars
Stripping off such disguise
As 'this will be' and 'this was.'
There is not another moment to lose.

An Enemy of the People

Chased down, and baited for the kill,
    And naked to men's eyes,
I struggled blindly a great while
    And bared my teeth with lies.

Yet civil fury made small show;
    Men did not scourge nor spit;
And some few chafed their hands to draw
    My body from the pit.

And some few brought me proofs enough
    That faith and love remain.
Yet all the stones are not so rough
    As I am rough with pain.

That I, who could with Timon's voice
    Have bitten through the grave,
Stand leashed and dumb, deprived of choice,
    Being Compassion's slave.

ELIZABETH JENNINGS

Elizabeth Jennings was born in 1926 and died in 2001. She worked as a librarian in the Oxford City library and then in publishing before becoming a full-time writer and, in particular, a poet. At Oxford, she read English at St Anne's College and her work appeared in three issues of *Oxford Poetry* (Blackwell's, 1948 to 1950). Her poems constituted the Fantasy Poets pamphlet Number One (1952); there followed *Poems* (1953), likewise from the Fantasy Press. Her *Selected Poems* appeared in 1979, with *Collected Poems: 1953-1985* in 1986, and *New Collected Poems* in 2002 (all from Carcanet). The three poems reprinted here are from *New Collected Poems,* courtesy of Carcanet Press and David Higham Associates, Ltd.

The Enemies

Last night they came across the river and
Entered the city. Women were awake
With lights and food. They entertained the band,
Not asking what the men had come to take
Or what strange tongue they spoke
Or why they came so suddenly through the land.

Now in the morning all the town is filled
With stories of the swift and dark invasion;
The women say that not one stranger told
A reason for his coming. The intrusion
Was not for devastation:
Peace is apparent still on hearth and field.

Yet all the city is a haunted place.
Man meeting man speaks cautiously. Old friends
Close up the candid looks upon their face.
There is no warmth in hands accepting hands;
Each ponders, 'Better hide myself in case
Those strangers have set up their homes in minds
I used to walk in. Better draw the blinds
Even if the strangers haunt in my own house.'

My Grandmother

She kept an antique shop – or it kept her.
Among Apostle spoons and Bristol glass,
The faded silks, the heavy furniture,
She watched her own reflection in the brass
Salvers and silver bowls, as if to prove
Polish was all, there was no need of love.

And I remember how I once refused
To go out with her, since I was afraid.
It was perhaps a wish not to be used
Like antique objects. Though she never said
That she was hurt, I still could feel the guilt
Of that refusal, guessing how she felt.

Later, too frail to keep a shop, she put
All her best things in one long narrow room.
The place smelt old, of things too long kept shut,
The smell of absences where shadows come
That can't be polished. There was nothing then
To give her own reflection back again.

And when she died I felt no grief at all,
Only the guilt of what I once refused.
I walked into her room among the tall
Sideboards and cupboards – things she never used
But needed; and no finger-marks were there,
Only the new dust falling through the air.

The Diamond Cutter

Not what the light will do but how he shapes it
And what particular colours it will bear,

And something of the climber's concentration
Seeing the white peak, setting the right foot there.

Not how the sun was plausible at morning
Nor how it was distributed at noon,

And not how much the single stone could show
But rather how much brilliance it would shun;

Simply a paring down, a cleaving to
One object, as the star-gazer who sees

One single comet polished by its fall
Rather than countless, untouched galaxies.

ADRIAN MITCHELL

Adrian Mitchell was born in 1932 and died in 2008. He flourished not only as a populist poet but in the world of political theatre, with his translation of Peter Weiss's *Marat/Sade* (Royal Shakespeare Company, London, 1964), his anti-imperialist *US* (Royal Shakespeare Company, 1968), and his *Tyger* (on William Blake, National Theatre, 1971). *Heart on the Left: Poems 1953-1984* appeared in 1987 (Bloodaxe), followed by several further volumes from 'the Shadow Poet Laureate'. At Oxford, he read English at Christ Church. His poems constituted the Fantasy Poets pamphlet Number Twenty Four (1955); he edited *Oxford Poetry* (with Richard Selig, 1955); and he was editor of *The Isis*. The three poems reprinted here are from *Heart on the Left*, courtesy of Adrian Mitchell's widow, Celia Hewitt.

Ten Ways to Avoid Lending Your Wheelbarrow to Anybody

1 *Patriotic*

May I borrow your wheelbarrow?
I didn't lay down my life in World War II
so that you could borrow my wheelbarrow.

2 *Snobbish*

May I borrow your wheelbarrow?
Unfortunately Samuel Beckett is using it.

3 *Overweening*

May I borrow your wheelbarrow?
It is too mighty a conveyance to be wielded
by any mortal save myself.

4 *Pious*

May I borrow your wheelbarrow?
My wheelbarrow is reserved for religious ceremonies.

5 *Melodramatic*

May I borrow your wheelbarrow?
I would sooner be broken on its wheel
and buried in its barrow.

6 *Pathetic*

May I borrow your wheelbarrow?
I am dying of schizophrenia
and all you can talk about is wheelbarrows.

7 *Defensive*

May I borrow your wheelbarrow?
Do you think I'm made of wheelbarrows?

8 *Sinister*

May I borrow your wheelbarrow?
It is full of blood.

9 *Lecherous*

May I borrow your wheelbarrow?
Only if I can fuck your wife in it.

10 *Philosophical*

May I borrow your wheelbarrow?
What is a wheelbarrow?

Time and Motion Study

Slow down the film. You see that bit.
Seven days old and no work done.
Two hands clutching nothing but air.
Two legs kicking nothing but air.
That yell. There's wasted energy there.
No use to himself, no good for the firm.
Make a note of that.

New film. Now look, now he's fourteen.
Work out the energy required
To make him grow that tall.
It could have been used
It could have all been used
For the good of the firm and he could have stayed small.
Make a note of that.

Age thirty. And the waste continues.
Using his legs for walking. Tiring
His mouth with talking and eating. Twitching.
Slow it down. Reproducing? I see.
All, I suppose, for the good of the firm.
But he'd better change methods. Yes, he'd better.
Look at the waste of time and emotion,
Look at the waste. Look. Look.
And make a note of that.

Remember Suez?

England, unlike junior nations,
Wears officers' long combinations.
So no embarrassment was felt
By the Church, the Government or the Crown.
But I saw the Thames like a grubby old belt
And England's trousers falling down.

JONATHAN PRICE

Jonathan Price was born in 1931 and died in 1985. At Oxford, he read English at Lincoln College, and he edited (with Anthony Thwaite, in 1954) *Oxford Poetry.* His poems constituted the Fantasy Press pamphlet Number Twenty (1954). His professional life was in publishing, from 1964 at Oxford University Press. His book of poems, *Everything Must Go* (Secker & Warburg,1985), of which he had seen early copies, appeared a month after his death. It carried a tribute from Philip Larkin: "Jonathan Price's poems are very much of his time in their form, but their wit and poignant feeling remain a unique achievement. This book will enable us to throw away the tattered cuttings we have kept so long." The three poems reprinted here are from *Everything Must Go,* courtesy of Joyce Lowrie Price.

A Considered Reply to a Child

'I love you', you said between two mouthfuls of pudding.
But not funny; I didn't want to laugh at all.
Rolling three years' experience in a ball,
You nudged it friendlily across the table.

A stranger, almost, I was flattered – no kidding.
It's not every day I hear a thing like that;
And when I do my answer's never pat.
I'm about nine times your age, ten times less able

To say – what you said; incapable of unloading
Plonk at someone's feet, like a box of bricks,
A declaration. When I try, it sticks
Like fish-bones in my throat; my eyes tingle.

What's called 'passion', you'll learn, may become 'overriding'.
But not in me it doesn't: I'm that smart,
I can give everything and keep my heart.
Kisses are kisses. No need for souls to mingle.

Bed's bed, what's more, and you'd say it's meant for sleeping;
And, believe me, you'd be absolutely right.
With luck you'll never lie awake all night,
Someone beside you (rather like 'crying') weeping.

Post Mortem

In fact I only met her once or twice
At parties and things, you know.
He was usually there too somewhere
Knocking back the old hard stuff.

I remember thinking she looked quite nice
But sort of not there, you know.
I mean she looked as if *you* weren't there
Or as if she'd had about enough

And wanted to get the hell out of it.
But I never thought she'd – you know.
Actually I'm surprised he had the face
To turn up as if everything was all right.

I mean there was no doubt about it,
Everyone knew they were – you know.
He was hardly ever at their place,
Or at least never stayed the night.

I remember one time she'd picked up a book
By some archaeologist, you know,
And she just sort of stood there staring
At one of those bodies they made at Pompeii

By filling up a hole. She had this look. . .
Someone might have guessed, you know.
Of course it's a bit late now to start caring
About her. But I pity him, I must say.

Night Thoughts

Things past include a boy dangling a string,
Baited with meat scraps, into a dark pool.
Harmless and unharmed, small crabs sidle round
The bottom of a can. The wind turns cool,
The crabs are counted and tipped back where found,
The boy runs home to tea. A timeless thing.

Things change in time: it's the crab's turn tonight.
It gorges now on liver, will move on
From that to who knows what, and won't be caught.
I launch pills down to stun it. It has gone.
It has not gone. I wonder if I ought
To turn us both off like a bedside light.

ANTHONY THWAITE

Anthony Thwaite was born in 1930. He has been a university teacher in Japan and Libya as well as in England, a producer at the BBC, literary editor of *The Listener* and *New Statesman*, and co-editor of *Encounter* (from 1973 to 1985). His *Selected Poems 1956-1996* appeared in 1997, and his *Collected Poems*, gathering a dozen volumes, in 2007 (both from Enitharmon Press). In 1999, Waywiser Press published *Anthony Thwaite in Conversation with Peter Dale and Ian Hamilton,* which presents a series of interviews attending to the poet's views of the art. At Oxford, he read English at Christ Church; his poems constituted the Fantasy Poets pamphlet Number Seventeen (1953), and he edited *Oxford Poetry* (with Jonathan Price, 1954) as well as editing *The Isis.* The three poems reprinted here are from *Collected Poems,* courtesy of Anthony Thwaite and of Enitharmon Press.

Death of a Rat

Nothing the critic said of tragedy,
Groomed for the stage and mastered into art,
Was relevant to this; yet I could see
Pity and terror mixed in equal part.
Dramatically, a farce right from the start,
Armed with a stick, a hairbrush and a broom,
Two frightened maladroits shut in one room.

Convenient symbol for a modern hell,
The long lean devil and the short squat man
No doubt in this were psychological,
Parable for the times, Hyperion
And Satyr, opposites in union . . .
Or Lawrence's *Snake,* to turn the picture round –
Man's pettiness by petty instinct bound.

But, to be honest, it was neither, and
That ninety minutes skirring in a duel
Was nothing if not honest. The demand
Moved him towards death, and me to play the fool,
Yet each in earnest. I went back to school
To con the hero's part, who, clung with sweat,
Learned where the hero, fool and coward met.

Curtain to bed and bed to corner, he
Nosed at each barrier, chattered, crouched, and then
Eluded me, till art and fear and pity
Offered him to me at the moment when
I broke his back, and smashed again, again,
Primitive, yes, exultant, yes, and knowing
His eyes were bright with some instinctive thing.

If every violent death is tragedy
And the wild animal is tragic most
When man adopts death's ingenuity,
Then this was tragic. But what each had lost
Was less and more than this, which was the ghost
Of some primeval joke, now in bad taste,
Which saw no less than war, no more than waste.

To My Unborn Child

Nothing is known but that you are
And move under her hand and mine,
Feeding and sleeping, clandestine
Agent and close conspirator.
You mould your own unique design
And grow frail roots nine months in her.

Collision of erratic spores
Moved eyes to bud, fingers to swell
Out of the light, and now he walks
On water, and is miracle.

What you will be the uncertain world
Waits for and watches, nor can make
Provision for each loose mistake
You drop when, far beyond the fold,
The days you pass, the routes you take
Teach you to be shy or bold.

The tent of flesh, the hut of bone
Shelter him on pilgrimage
And blood and water build for him
A flooded road, a shifting bridge.

Not yet real, we make for you
A toy that is reality.
The secret country where you lie
Is far from it, but no less true,
And both are dangerous to the eye
That fears what flesh and fate may do.

Tent, hut, and bridge are weak as he
And yet unnumbered travellers
Have spent dark nights encamped in such
Retreats, and trod such paths as hers.

You who will soon step down through blood
To where earth, sky and air combine
To make you neither hers nor mine,
Think: you now stand where many stood
Who, each in his own unique design,
Was weak and strong and bad and good.

And yet these murmurs cannot break
The doors which you alone unbar,
And we who know all this must know
Nothing is known but that you are.

Mr Cooper

Two nights in Manchester: nothing much to do,
One of them I spent partly in a pub,
Alone, quiet, listening to people who
Didn't know me. *So I told the bloody sub-*
Manager what he could do with it. . . . Mr Payne
Covers this district – you'll have met before?
Caught short, I looked for the necessary door
And moved towards it; could hear, outside, the rain.

The usual place, with every surface smooth
To stop, I suppose, the aspirations of
The man with pencil stub and dreams of YOUTH
AGED 17. And then I saw, above
The stall, a card, a local jeweller's card
Engraved with name, JEWELLER AND WATCHMENDER
FOR FIFTY YEARS, address, telephone number.
I heard the thin rain falling in the yard.

The card was on a sort of shelf, just close
Enough to let me read this on the front.
Not, I'd have said, the sort of words to engross
Even the keenest reader, nothing to affront
The public decency of Manchester.
And yet I turned it over. On the back
Were just three words in rather smudgy black
Soft pencil: MR COOPER – DEAD. The year

Grew weakly green outside, in blackened trees,
Wet grass by statues. It was ten to ten
In March in Manchester. Now, ill at ease
And made unsure of sense and judgement when
Three words could throw me, I walked back into
The bar, where nothing much had happened since
I'd left. A man was trying to convince
Another man that somehow someone knew

Something that someone else had somehow done.
Two women sat and drank the lagers they
Were drinking when I'd gone. If anyone
Knew I was there, or had been, or might stay,
They didn't show it. *Good night,* I almost said,
Went out to find the rain had stopped, walked back
To my hotel, and felt the night, tall, black,
Above tall roofs. And Mr Cooper dead.

A NOTE ABOUT CHRISTOPHER RICKS

Christopher Ricks was elected Professor of Poetry at Oxford in 2004. He is the William M. and Sara B. Warren Professor of the Humanities, and Co-Director of the Editorial Institute, at Boston University, having formerly been Professor of English at Bristol and at Cambridge. He was President of the Association of Literary Scholars, Critics, and Writers, 2007-2008. For services to scholarship he was knighted in 2009. The editor of *The Poems of Tennyson* (3 vols., 1987), *The New Oxford Book of Victorian Verse* (1987), *Inventions of the March Hare: Poems 1909-1917 by T.S. Eliot* (1996), *The Oxford Book of English Verse* (1999), *Selected Poems of James Henry* (2002), and Samuel Menashe's *New and Selected Poems* (2005), he is the author of *Milton's Grand Style* (1963), *Keats and Embarrassment* (1974), *The Force of Poetry* (1984), *T.S. Eliot and Prejudice* (1988), *Tennyson* (1989), *Beckett's Dying Words* (1993), *Essays in Appreciation* (1996), *Allusion to the Poets* (2002), *Reviewery* (2002), *Decisions and Revisions in T.S. Eliot* (2003), *Dylan's Visions of Sin* (2004), and *True Friendship: Geoffrey Hill, Anthony Hecht, and Robert Lowell under the Sign of Eliot and Pound* (2010).

Other books from Waywiser

POETRY

Al Alvarez, *New & Selected Poems*
Robert Conquest: *Penultimata*
Morri Creech, *Field Knowledge*
Peter Dale, *One Another*
Erica Dawson, *Big-Eyed Afraid*
B. H. Fairchild, *The Art of the Lathe*
Jeffrey Harrison, *The Names of Things: New & Selected Poems*
Joseph Harrison, *Identity Theft*
Joseph Harrison, *Someone Else's Name*
Anthony Hecht, *Collected Later Poems*
Anthony Hecht, *The Darkness and the Light*
Carrie Jerrell, *After the Revival*
Rose Kelleher, *Bundle o' Tinder*
Dora Malech, *Shore Ordered Ocean*
Eric McHenry, *Potscrubber Lullabies*
Timothy Murphy, *Very Far North*
Ian Parks, *Shell Island*
Chris Preddle, *Cattle Console Him*
Daniel Rifenburgh, *Advent*
W.D. Snodgrass: *Not for Specialists: New & Selected Poems**
Mark Strand, *Blizzard of One**
Bradford Gray Telford: *Perfect Hurt*
Cody Walker, *Shuffle and Breakdown*
Deborah Warren, *The Size of Happiness*
Clive Watkins, *Jigsaw*
Richard Wilbur, *Mayflies**
Richard Wilbur, *Collected Poems 1943-2004*
Norman Williams, *One Unblinking Eye*
Greg Williamson, *A Most Marvelous Piece of Luck*

FICTION

Gregory Heath, *The Entire Animal*
Matthew Yorke, *Chancing It*

ILLUSTRATED

Nicholas Garland, *I wish ...*

NON-FICTION

Neil Berry, *Articles of Faith: The Story of British Intellectual Journalism*
Mark Ford, *A Driftwood Altar: Essays and Reviews*
Richard Wollheim, *Germs: A Memoir of Childhood*

*Expanded UK edition